DON'T GIVE UP BEFORE THE MIRACLE HAPPENS

A RELATIONSHIP GUIDEBOOK FOR SAME-SEX COUPLES

Author

WARRICK T. STEWART

S&D Enterprises
Publishing Company

Copyright © 2015 by Dr. Warrick T. Stewart.

Published by S&D Enterprises, Atlanta, Georgia.

All rights reserved. No part of this publication may be reproduced, stored in a retrieval system, or transmitted in any form or by any means, electronic, mechanical, photocopying, recording, scanning, or otherwise, except as permitted under Section 107 or 108 of the 1976 Copyrights Act, without either the prior written permission of the Publisher, or authorization through payment of the appropriate per-copy fee at www.copyright.com.

Requests to the Publisher for permission should be addressed to the Permissions Department at S&D Enterprises at 3855 Shallowford Road, Ste. 515, Atlanta, GA 30062.

In memory of all of the men and women whose stories want be told due to senseless hate and violence.

Introduction

If you, like many people, worry about the state of your committed relationship, you are not alone. This modern age is a scary time for the success of relationships. From low morals in society to rampant temptations that assail us from different angles, plus a "me first" culture, it's a surprise some relationships actually last! The high rate of divorce is even more so frightening due to how nobody, including some experts, seem to comprehend why relationships that started up with so much promise end up failing miserably.

Despite these dire statistics, there is no reason you can't reap the joys of a loving committed relationship. No matter what your background or current state, with the right mindset and approach, such as those I've tackled in this book, you and your partner can overcome many relationship challenges.

As someone who survived a childhood that was bereft of companionship and acceptance and has today grown into an adult who enjoys a fulfilling long-term relationship, I can attest that happiness with a special someone is very much possible. From a lonely past filled with longing and acceptance, I walk today on a path blessed with strength and personal satisfaction. I spend my days advocating for those who, like me, have lived through difficult times, have felt deep sadness and self-hate. I speak out publicly for my brothers and sisters, and my hope is to help them find peace, love, and acceptance in their adult lives. At its core, my hope is to help them, and anyone who have once spoken the language of longing and grief, find a new way to live.

It is in adversary that you, as an individual and as part of a romantic duo, grow and learn. If you currently find yourself in the midst of a troubled relationship, it may seem like it is over. Have faith. You are not alone. While you are a unique person capable of love and deserving of love, your relationship problems aren't as rare as you may believe. Nor are they invincible.

Using the wealth of information I have gathered in more than six years of work I've conducted as a psychotherapist and Life Coach, plus my own intensive experience from my current eight-year relationship, I have put together a catalog of marital tips. The wealth of information held in this book has greatly benefitted my own committed relationship, as well as those experienced by the hundreds of couples I have counselled.

I look back on my own difficult past experiences with contentment in my heart. The sorrows of my past have transformed me into the strong person I am today. The hardships I've encountered – in my tumultuous childhood and in my own relationships – have provided me with the unparalleled lessons I constantly tap into to help other people who are going through their own struggles, as individuals and as someone's romantic partner.

Read through and contemplate on the tips taught and carefully collected in this book and you, too, will one day be able to look back and have a grateful heart towards the relationship problems you currently face. Here you may not find a shortcut or one solitary key that holds the promise of a perfect love, but I assure you that these are tried-and-tested methods that will provide your relationship with solid footing and a fighting chance. There are no gimmicks or manipulation tactics outlined in this book, no sneaky tactics that may get you want you desire in the interim with your partner but will eventually prove inimical and counterproductive.

Instead, what I've outlined here are fundamental and specific approaches you can take for the betterment of your relationship. From explicit approaches to better the communication that transpires between you and your mate, to boundaries you can set that encourage mutual respect, to avoiding common relationship pitfalls like nagging and more, what you hold in your hand are steps that will not only give your relationship a sturdy fighting chance, they will raise the intimacy and joy you and your partner receive from one another.

Don't give up before the miracles happen in your relationship. I commend you for making the choice of picking up this book. It means you haven't turned your back on your relationship and you're taking matters in your own hands. It is in accepting the fact that we can only control our own actions that we can actually impact our current situations and create an opportunity for lifelong change.

Whatever knowledge you can absorb from this book, I hope and pray you pass it on to others. In the words of St. Francis, it is in giving that we receive. It is my utmost desire that when you've completed this book, you will be armed with detailed steps to help you deal with your partner in a more loving and accepting way. It is in approaching life with the mindset of acceptance, hope and love that we can rise above any problem and continue to grow into the persons we were meant to be.

All the best,

DON'T GIVE UP BEFORE THE MIRACLE HAPPENS

A RELATIONSHIP GUIDEBOOK FOR SAME-SEX COUPLES

Tip 1: Say what you mean, and mean what you say

"Love is like the truth, sometimes it prevails, and sometimes it hurts."
—Victor M. Garcia Jr.

Communication between two people in a relationship is no easy feat and that is why saying what we mean, and meaning what we say is so important. With our words and body language, we can relay a wide array of emotions. And if getting the right words and signals across is difficult enough, - especially after a grueling day at work, or having to deal with some adults temper tantrum, - factor in misunderstandings and it's easy to see why communication breakdown is too common in relationships. The good news is that great communication can be learned. Effort and understanding, as well as patience, will have to come into play. Like all vital learning experiences, there is a steep learning curve, and some days are just a lot more difficult than others.

Communication is not just about learning to say the right words - doing so, of course, is paramount in effective communication - but also learning when to be silent and being a good listener. Wives and husbands are apt to complain about their spouses not being attentive enough. It's not just painful verbal daggers that prove damaging to relationships.

Being inattentive, or even just seeming to be, can be as destructive as swear words and other insults.

In such a hectic world, people fall into the habit of drowning their spouses out, even if it's not a deliberate choice. When emotions fog your mind, you can forget the fact that your spouse is the most important person in your life, the one who should be getting the most respect from you. The amount of work you dedicate in bettering communication in your relationship will pay you and your family back tenfold.

Learn how you can be a much better listener. Listening is a skill any wife or husband will be sure to appreciate. How can you listen without judgment? What verbal and non-verbal cues can you provide your spouse to make them feel positive and loved? How can any wife or husband feel comfortable enough to be honest, while respecting the dignity of the other person, and not have the conversation turn into a heated argument? Work diligently on your communication techniques and watch your relationship improve beyond what anyone would expect.

Be an Active Listener

Effective communication does not simply know which words to employ. Next in line knows how to be an active listener. Active listening goes beyond passive aggressive replies that hide your true feelings, simply to keep the peace at home. Examples include saying *yes* when your innermost soul is screaming *no*. Active listening takes a step over and above keeping the status quo - it's validating your partner in a healthy and loving way that relays to them that they are being heard and acknowledged.

For instance, if your wife tells you she was feeling sick at work and how you didn't offer to pick up the children from school, instead of brushing her off with a curt reply or, worse, picking a fight because you just had to explain how much tougher your day was, active listening is telling your beloved, in a loving tone, something along the lines of, "I believe you're saying that you were having a terrible day and it would have taken a load off your shoulders had I volunteered to get the children. Is that what you're trying to say?"

This type of response validates her feelings and tells her that you acknowledge her emotions. Listening attentively is a very strong expression of love in itself. Offering a hug immediately afterwards, or some other form of physical affection while maintaining eye contact, will then tell your significant other that you not only heard the words coming out of their mouth, you truly feel and care for them.

In a healthy relationship, one where two people make an effort to love each other despite any fleeting feelings, the couple chooses to ignore reacting defensively to criticisms. Instead, they find ways to express love and support.

Difficult Conversations

Plenty of people avoid difficult conversations, while some thrive on drama. If you're one of the latter, get rid of drama-inducing habits as much as you can. Arguing regularly, including fighting over small matters, builds up to frustration, lack of trust, deeper anger and resentments in relationships.

Nobody can avoid difficult conversations, especially in a relationship that's supposed to last for decades. Knowing how to bring up sensitive issues is a must, as well as knowing when to let the small things slide, no matter how annoyed you may feel about a particular episode. Not every battle has to be fought. Never forget how you and your spouse are on the same team.

As for tough conversations that need to be dealt with, here are some useful tips to help you converse with your spouse and not end up screaming at each other, or engaging in a silent war:

Feelings aren't always facts. Needless to say, feelings are tremendously important. When two people love each other, they must work very hard at valuing the feelings of their mate. When it comes to communicating, often times it's our own blown up feelings that make us difficult to deal with. Tough conversations in relationship don't necessarily involve supremely important topics. It could be as mundane as feeling hurt and rejected because your husband didn't answer his phone right away. Or feeling enraged because your wife forgot to run the errand she promised she'd take care of. People make mistakes. People get busy. Not every hurt feeling of yours means your spouse doesn't love you. Tackle any issues after you put your ego aside and put your negative feelings into proper perspective. Think before you speak. This cliché will always hold true, especially within what should be the most important relationship of your life.

Ensure both you and your spouse are prepared for what could be a less-than-pleasant conversation. Bringing up a sensitive topic while your partner is relaxing is never a good idea. Neither is it healthy to tell your wife or husband that you have to have "a talk" the night before they're about to start a new job. And the art of tackling a tough subject matter goes beyond good timing. Specifically setting a time to talk with your spouse without unreasonable demands will help them prepare for the conversation while allowing them to choose when the exchange will occur. This way, when you do talk about whatever issue is at hand, you will be both mentally and physically prepared.

When in doubt, remember that a kind word, most especially one that involves you swallowing a big gulp of bitter pride, will tremendously benefit your relationship in the long run. A hurtful reply might satisfy an ephemeral feeling but the consequences can leave devastated lives in its wake.

Tip 2: Always make time for each other and your relationship

"If you want to go quickly, go alone. If you want to go far, go together."
—African proverb

How much of your day do you think you spend in communication with others? Most people don't realize that the average adult spends 70% of their time communicating with other people. When you remove the amount of time spent sleeping, this is a staggering amount of your waking hours. With almost a constant exchange of communication, sometimes we can fall victim to not devoting the time and effort necessary to maintain effective, positive, and healthy communication with our spouse.

Our usual communication is filled with a lot of informational and cursory interaction, but informational communication and cursory interactions cannot fulfill the emotional needs of yourself and your spouse. This is why it's important in a relationship to set aside time and effort to create a space for honest and meaningful conversation. Sometimes "How was your day?" over dinner and under the sound of the evening news just isn't enough.

Make Time for Multiple Kinds of Intimacy

Slipping into patterns is a natural human behavior. In

relationship, we need to make sure those habits do not create a void of intimacy—that we don't fall into patterns of formality and distance. Just like a leaky faucet, if you don't make time to maintain and fix intimacy in your relationship, you allow the union to fill with a gulf of emotional distance.

There are many kinds of intimacy in a relationship and not all kinds of intimacy are emphasized. Part of making time for your spouse is working with them to develop intimacy in areas such as parenting, social lives, recreation and hobbies, and even finances.

Lasting relationships are supported by two people who are friends, share similar financial goals, and continue to feel attracted and drawn to their spouse. If sharing similar goals is a foundation stone of relationship, then making time to create intimacy to discuss finances, vacations, careers, and parenting ideas is an important key to a relationship that continues to fulfill both your needs.

Building Romance

Another trap created from the daily grind of the work schedule and family time is the ebbing of that romantic spark. Every flame will sputter and flicker from time to time, but in your relationship, it's vital that you never allow the fire to be extinguished.

An easy way to keep the flame of romance alive is to find time to play. Household chores and the latest memo from your boss don't leave a lot of time for levity. Levity and flirtation with your spouse is a necessary part of the romantic experience. Revive an old inside joke from your early days together. Find a way to brighten the monotonous grays that dull our days. Inject humor and color in the mundane.

When you can introduce a playful spirit, then finding the time to have a romantic evening or moment comes naturally. The best way to fight any awkward feelings of trying to "force romance" is to make it light and playful. Flirting and a playful spirit are incubators of romance and love—it's where you stood when you first started dating each other, so why can't you use that in relationship?

It's also important to be honest and share your romantic notes in a positive way with your mate. Honesty reciprocates honesty in a healthy relationship. By sharing what you want, you encourage the same from your spouse. When your spouse listens to your feelings and needs, you express and fulfill your own wants and needs. You end up activating a natural endorphin-rush in your mind as a result of loving reciprocation.

Finally, when you take time for romance, it's important to express appreciation of your partner's efforts, be they mountains or molehills.

Earnest gratitude is a bridge to emotional openness and intimacy. By taking time from your schedule as a couple to allow romance to flourish, you are maintaining a healthy foundation for your relationship.

Finding Time for One Another

So, how can you find time for intimacy and romance in your busy schedules? If you cannot seem to find time for yourselves in a crazy, fast-paced modern life, how can you even think about romance and intimacy?

The simplest and most repeatable advice I've ever received is to always plan something in advance. Having something to look forward to as a couple will strengthen your emotional connection. It fortifies intimacy. Spontaneity can be magical, but often times in a relationship between two busy people, it can be unrealistic and even stressful.

Springing a date night may interfere with your spouses plans and schedule for the week—thereby creating even more stress. Instead, find time together to regularly plan a simple retreat. Retreat does not mean running off somewhere all the time, instead think of a retreat as an elimination of distractions. It could simply be eating dinner together without the kids, without the TV, allowing you time to just be together, Be a couple. It's during these times that you can work on sharing intimacy together and kindling romance.

The first stepping-stone to improving your relationship is putting forth a regular effort to create meaningful time together. Put the first foot forward and carve out time with your spouse, create a safe space and a safe time to build on the positive things your relationship brings - be it support, empathy, and honest intimacy. And most importantly remember that "if you want to go quickly, go alone. If you want to go far, go together."

Tip 3: We all fight - but learn to fight fair.

"An eye for an eye will only make the whole world blind."
— Mahatma Gandhi

Conflicts are an inevitable facet of relationships that can become magnified especially in relationships. They arise out of difference of needs. In a relationship, we need to feel comfortable, supported, and understood by the person with whom we are most intimate in the world. When our expectations of these needs are not met, when they are unrealistic or are perceived differently by our spouse, conflict can begin to take over in the relationship.

Conflict in a relationship is more than a simple misunderstanding or disagreement. If one person perceives a threat, whether real or not, then there will be conflict. What do we mean by threat? A threat can be any anticipated attack on a vulnerable part of the mind and emotions. Threats, in turn, trigger strong emotional reactions. How you manage these emotional reactions when you feel vulnerable and threatened is how you handle conflicts.

Perhaps above all, in a relationship it is important to maintain a level playing field. There can be no tolerance for "fighting dirty." Undercutting your spouse with a cheap and petty trick designed specifically to hit a weak point only you can know doesn't win you the argument; it loses your relationship.

Love is War

We've all heard the phrase "lose the battle; win the war" and love is often called war. The constant refrain being "all's fair in love and war." A good general will sacrifice a battle to gain a strategic advantage for a later date. But, in a relationship, this approach is not a winning tactic. It's nothing short of sabotage.

By 'saving up' mistakes your spouse makes to be used at a later date, or keeping count for your personal advantage, does not help your relationship. Instead, you're opening old wounds and preventing them from healing. Wounds that never heal become scars, and the bitter scars from an unhappy relationship will never fade.

Remember, in war the goal is to destroy your opponent or force them to surrender. Love is not war. Nor should be your relationship.

The Silent Treatment

There's a school of thought that advocates the silent treatment in conflict. Withdraw from explosive, angry, and hurtful shouting and reactions into a frigid but not scathing silence. Wait for the tide of tempers to go out and allow cooler heads to prevail.

The truth behind the silent treatment is that it's perhaps more painful than a heated argument. There's a reason why prisons use solitary confinement as a punishment: it's the isolation. By giving your spouse the 'silent treatment' you're isolating them. You're allowing the hurt and pain from conflict to ferment and punish them further. To resolve a conflict seek compromise, not further punishment.

Taking a direct approach to conflict can save your relationship before it's ever in jeopardy. Evading a disagreement is born out of fear - fear of being wrong, fear of being misunderstood, and fear of vulnerability. The silent treatment is a simple evasion tactic. If you want to have a fair, and open resolution with your spouse the silent treatment is directly detrimental to the resolution and healing process.

Healthy Resolution

The first step to fairly and openly resolving a conflict is to acknowledge the disagreement, the difference of needs and expectations, and listen. Dismissive behavior is one of the most psychologically damaging behaviors for one person to another. Acknowledge, listen, and put yourself in their shoes for a moment.

Taking pause to try to gain an insight into your partner's perspective will help take the edge off the stress. Stress is the first enemy in a conflict. A conflict in a relationship is highly stressing. The best answer is to relax and try to ease the stress of your partner. High stress levels will inhibit your ability to see to the root of the issue, it'll interfere with your reading of the other person's non-verbal communication, and it will even obscure your own feelings. Learn how to rapidly relieve stress, not just for yourself but for your spouse too.

Second, you need to activate your emotional awareness. You need to understand precisely how you feel in order to communicate your needs and resolve the disagreement. When you're capable of understanding your emotions you open yourself to empathy and being able to sense how your spouse is feeling. Understanding paves the way for resolution.

Finally, utilize humor. A single moment of levity, of joy, can undo stress, open up closed off emotions, and reduce tension. Humor can put the disagreement in unexpected perspective. Why were we arguing over this anyways? That single moment of joy can lead to the final opportunity afforded by conflict: the opportunity to grow and build stronger trust. If you can make a joke about an angry moment, you can feel secure in knowing that your relationship has reached the point where it will survive unexpected adversity and disagreement.

Conflicts in relationship run deeper than just a simple

disagreement. The grooves of your character are as familiar to your spouse as any part of your physical appearance. When these grooves go against each other, strong emotions can be triggered and fester if untended. Taking a proactive, positive, and honest approach to conflict resolution will result in an opportunity to strengthen your relationship, to improve the feeling of security and trust leaving it stronger than it was before.

Tip 4: Stay committed

"When you like someone, you like them in spite of their faults. When you love someone, you love them with their faults."
—Elizabeth Cameron

Have you ever stopped to wonder where your relationship is going and rather you have the commitment to withstand the challenges that are sure to come? Will it be happiness or misery? Will there be plenty of excitement or doldrums? Will it be a lifetime of partnership and love or will it end quickly with a messy divorce?

Successful relationships are said to have been created in heaven, or simply a case of finding that one perfect partner. Sure, these statements contain grains of truth, but they can also be mere exaggerations. A happy and contented life is the result of hard work, the product of two people making the commitment to stick through life's ups and downs and not giving up before the miracle happens, which isn't always easy.

In America today, there are over 100 million unmarried adults, making up almost half the relationship-appropriate population, in terms of age. To meet potential partners, many - I'm talking millions of people - register on dating websites to meet someone. Although lots of single individuals - and, sadly, not-so-single people - are on the look out for a relationship, although the million dollar question is "how many people of these people, are ready to go the extra mile to become the right man or woman for someone?" Being committed in a relationship forces us to love our partners in spite of their faults, because when you love someone, you love them with their faults.

The Keyword is Commitment

Commitment is not a very sexy word but it is absolutely necessary in making any relationship a success. Love is the quintessential element that binds us to make a lifelong commitment to another. Love, and the subsequent commitment involved, is more than a whirlwind of emotions, like the thrills spectators experience from watching a TV series, or the turbulent lovers depicted in films. It's more than the tender plight of protagonists found in bestselling romance novels. Feelings are sensations that come and go, highly ephemeral. Commitment, on the other hand, is a true decision that should last over the years, breaking through whirlwind of emotions.

Why is commitment important? The word *commitment* is not stated in a typical western relationship vow, nor is it printed on a relationship license. Commitment is vital because it involves a couple who acts in a proactive manner, knowing how important commitment's role is in binding a future together. Commitment is a pledge to stay and work together, side by side, through the years. Commitment doesn't say "Only for today" - it firmly proclaims, "Through thick and thin."

Five signs of Commitment in a Relationship

Are you committed to your relationship? Commitment is like dancing the tango, you need your partner's cooperation in executing all those twists and turns. Commitment is not the decision of one individual making up all the rules. Two people must mutually agree to share a future together, a future that involves compromise and open discussions.

1. **Loving and respecting each other.** In love that lasts, accepting your partner's feelings and goals is important. Being committed doesn't mean ignoring your spouse's hopes and dreams, especially those that contradict your own. Although two people share a life in relationship, each must retain his or her individuality to a certain healthy degree.

2. **Being loyal and honest while trusting each other.** Relationship minus loyalty is like a broken violin, a beautiful instrument that no longer produces the sublime music it was built to emit. Without trust and loyalty, no relationship can last.

3. **Being there for each other.** It's not the length of time you share but the quality of your moments together. Do you support each other through the different stages of your lives, in all ways you can, through good times and times of crisis?

4. **Working on a harmonious and loving home.** The decision to live together is a big one. There are plenty of pros and cons when it comes to living together. In a relationship, people have to share responsibilities including financial ones, child-rearing and countless others. Adjustments will have to be made by each person. Committed spouses make a deliberate decision to meet each other halfway.

5. **Owning mutual assets.** This is one of the highest points in making a commitment. Financial investments made with your mate are giant leaps toward an embankment in the next level of your relationship.

Building Commitment in Your Relationship

Through life's stages, great and awful moments, your commitment to each other should not falter. Your feelings will, expect that much. A conscious decision, on the other hand, is not based on feelings alone. Your relationship is an exotic plant that needs plenty of care, attention and hard work in order to thrive. When things are rosy, commitment is easy, but real life will bring in tough times.

Here are ways you can improve commitment within your relationship:

1. **Prioritize your relationship.** Make sure that your relationship is one of the most important things in your life. Respect and love your mate and give them importance in your day-to-day life. Don't expect a happy relationship that will survive the years when you prepare an expensive anniversary vacation each year but don't make time for your spouse on a regular basis.

2. **Spend fun times together, plenty of fun times.** Your time is an invaluable gift you can give to your partner. No matter how busy you are, find time to relax and relish in the wonderful traits of your partner. Congratulate each other on achievements grand and small.

3. **Never ever cheat.** This sounds like advice that doesn't need to be uttered but loyalty and commitment must always go hand in hand, that cannot be stressed enough. You can't have commitment when you don't work hard at staying loyal. This includes staying away from situations that most people would consider unsafe, as far as romantic relationships are concerned. A night out at a strip club can and will damage trust. Chatting up your ex when your husband makes you feel ignored is asking for trouble. Go the extra mile and avoid exposing yourself to sensual

pleasures that would hurt your partner.

4. **Seek advice to better your relationship.** Whether your relationship is in a stable phase or sinking in troubled waters, you should always make use of all the options available to better your lifelong commitment. There's an infinite amount to learn when it comes to bettering relationships.

5. **Be the initiator.** Don't let your commitment depend on the other person's commitment. Unless there's any form of abuse involved, in which case you must immediately seek help and a safe refuge away from your spouse, do your part to be a more loving person without keeping tabs on your spouse's efforts. Continue to keep the fires burning in your relationship by taking charge of your own actions. Any romance can shine through the darkest night when both individuals make a habit of initiating love and light in their relationship.

When two people who love each other are both willing to go through the ups and downs of life as a team, their relationship has a great shot at lasting through life's waves. Commitment is a decision that should be made every single day. It's hard work that will bring your relationship joy, peace, laughter and the most wonderful memories.

Tip 5: Learn to appreciate your partner on a deeper level

"A friend is one that knows you as you are, understands where you have been, accepts what you have become, and still, gently allows you to grow."
—William Shakespeare

Loving your partner on a deeper level sounds like the ultimate rule in making a relationship successful. In reality, a better and happier relationship is built on many glorious things. Love is the end all and be all, but "loving your mate" sounds too general. Love also means many various things to different people. Love can be romantic, friendly, or all about feelings, depending on how you define love. I've heard stories of people who claim they love their partners but they don't feel the same passion towards one another, not in the way they did in the budding stage of their relationship. One thing is clear - love without actions is empty. One of the best ways to show your love for another is by demonstrating gratitude regularly. The feeling of being appreciated is so amazing that it can even bring passion back to your relationship. Learning to share your appreciation for your spouse on a daily basis and reciprocating this adulation goes far in any relationship.

With dull wheels turning in daily existence, anyone can fall into routine, routine that leads to married people taking each other for granted. Being a victim of routine can be such a cunning and seemingly innocuous experience that often times couples forget to even say "thank you" to one another. And then they wonder why their relationship is falling apart!

This is a fast-paced world. Plenty of people concentrate too much on results rather than the effort the other person is providing, ignoring our partner's time and thoughtfulness. The negative things are noticed before the hard work provided by our mates. Because you can get used to having your partner around, you may end up focusing on things that irritate and hurt. This type of thinking is harmful to any relationship. Gratitude can turn the tide in a relationship that's headed south.

Here are ways to show appreciation to your spouse:

1. **Use creativity when saying thank you.** Use different phrases aside from "thank you", although these words should never be forgotten. Words like "I appreciate it when you…" or "I love it when you…" are magical. Leave a note, or at times when you're away from each other, mail a handwritten romantic letter to your spouse, one that focuses on gratitude and the things your partner does that you love. In a life of emails and text messages, handwritten notes can be more important than store-bought gifts.

2. **Include small but significant gestures to your day-to-day routine.** As the old adage says, big things come in small packages. In relationship, your partner will likely remember all the small things you do habitually, over occasional grand gestures. Lovingly greet each other after a day at work. Compliment your partner for simply smelling great. Give each other praises for little things. The fact that you noticed them will be appreciated, resulting in double gratitude in your relationship. How wonderful is that! The other route, the one that involves constant criticism, is one of the common reasons relationships fall apart. Focusing on what's positive, instead of what bothers you, will improve your relationship in more ways than you can count.

3. **Prepare loving meals for your spouse.** If you're an absolute disaster in the kitchen, make dining out a pleasurable habit. Get creative and find ways to relax together. Breaking bread is one of the easiest and quickest ways to show how much your partner means to you. Whenever the opportunity comes, go on a date with your spouse. Ask them for special dinner requests. Remember your first years together, those times when you both placed plenty of effort to make the other feel special. Tap into those old feelings and you'll be motivated to bond with your spouse over special meals. Whenever possible, spend some time out

without the kids. You deserve the relaxing time with one another.

4. **Do a chore you don't usually do for your mate.** Warm up their car before they head out to work. Offer to do chores your partner hates doing. His or her face will be sure to light up. The task can be as simple yet intimate as giving them a shave or a massage.

5. **Keep a gratitude journal and allow your spouse to read some parts of it.** Write down things you love about your spouse. Write down grateful thoughts on life in general, even things outside your relationship. Being a grateful person as a whole will translate to becoming a grateful partner yourself. Also, having your life partner know that they're one of the things you appreciate in life will make them feel valued - a very, very special feeling.

6. **Listen with your full attention.** Effective communication in relationship involves not just talking the right way, but also actively listening to what your spouse says. When we feel listened to and have our emotions validated, we feel loved and appreciated. Turn off all forms of communications and set aside other distractions when you're loved one is talking, especially when it's about issues that really matter to them. There's nothing like the feeling that you can be open to your partner.

7.   **Tell your friends how great your spouse is.** Complimenting your mate in front of your friends is not just about letting your spouse know they're adored or showing. Your friends, too, will benefit from the kind words and relationship modeling. Words of appreciation create a secure and loving atmosphere. Appreciative gestures provide children with a sense of appreciation towards other people, as they'll learn to copy how you and your mate interact together.

8.   **Praise your spouse in public.** It won't hurt to take advantage of technology. Take it to social media. Brag about your spouse and let your family and friends know how much you adore your other half. Do bring up your partner's accomplishments in front of family and friends.

9.   **Plan surprises regularly.** What better way to make your spouse feel deeply appreciated while bringing spice back to your relationship than providing delightful surprises throughout each year. Sspontaneity can be the main ingredient that saves a relationship. Booty-call your spouse by putting up an inviting sign on your bedroom door.

10.   **Be of service when your partner needs your care the most.** One of the best ways to make your other half feel special is by going out of your way when they need help. You are best friends as much

as you're married to each other, remember that. Rather than wait to be asked, offer to run errands when you can, especially when your husband or wife is extra stressed. Offer a massage, or allow them a long nap while you take care of chores. A rubdown after a long day says thank you in a way no words can.Expressing gratitude can truly make a tremendous difference in a relationship. There's joy in saying and hearing thank you, both through words and loving deeds. At the end of the day, you're with that person you vowed to love through thick and thin. What's a little thank you, anyway? Showing your partner gratitude may sound so simple but it does great miracles in all relationships.

Tip 6: Maintain a Sense of Humor

"Speaking with kindness creates confidence, thinking with kindness creates profoundness, giving with kindness creates love."
—Lao Tseu

A life partner is a help mate, best friend, lover, counsel and more; one that is meant to travel your life journey with you. As you walk hand in hand along this journey, certain challenges will be sure to creep upon the way.

We develop specific and personal coping mechanisms to help us deal with the circumstances dealt to us in life. These coping mechanisms, whether they're healthy or not, is part of the process of growing older. You might have gotten better over the years at managing your own struggles, but as you enter the covenant of relationship, it's a completely different picture. You now have to consider another individual's decisions in life. It can definitely be a tough battle at times because you were both raised in different environments. You have two people who grew up in separate homes, with varying values and past experiences, who now have to live together under one room for years to come. You and your spouse have developed separate ways of coping with life, ways that were developed way before the wedding day. Now you need to work things out as a team. Differences, when not handled properly, can create holes in your relationship - holes that lead to the decay and decline of any relationship.

We have often heard that laughter is the best medicine. It is indeed not just a medicine for curing illnesses, but a vitamin for preventing emotional woes, including relationship issues. It is always wise to maintain a sense of humor in your relationship. Lightening up will make you better company and a better partner. Laughing makes life exciting. Humor makes ordinary days occasions to look forward to.

Laughter releases endorphins from our bodies, natural feel-good chemicals that make us feel joy and energy. These happy chemicals can even help the circulation of blood in our bodies and may also prevent the clogging of arteries, plus other heart problems. Laughter can strengthen the immune systems, allowing us to cope with stress better. It can even increase our tolerance for pain and provide us with the power to heal at a cellular level. A minute of anger can swiftly weaken the body while a minute of laughter can boost feelings of happiness and our immune system.

As the years, or even months, roll by, you and your partner will begin to realize the fact that you're two different people who came together and brought separate worlds into one home. Each one of you is trying to plant your own personal flag inside a single abode. The butterflies in your tummy that used to signal romance will at times disappear; butterflies are, after all, known to have a short life span. Often times, in your daily existence, you and your partner will feel bored and irritated over small things- little things that your mate does can gnaw at you incessantly.

Whatever fantasy existed has turned into reality. The reality can often be a dull one. Daily life is now tiring - going to work, traveling back home, performing household chores and other repetitive tasks. Yet all these things won't morph into a big deal if you find something to laugh about together. Your partner should be considered as your closest friend, someone to enjoy life with, someone to share funny quips with. Make an effort to find fun things to do together, as well as fun ways to look at life.

It's not always about going out and spending money. Finding ways to make your partner smile is a priceless endeavor. Exert effort to bring color to your conversations. The more you get to know each other, the more you'll discover what your spouse's brand of humor is. Use this for the betterment of your relationship. Laughter creates a strong bond with those whom we laugh with. Humor helps us cope with things, as it clears our minds of unnecessary worries while making us think better and handle things efficiently.

Laughing beats being miserable or too high-strung. Plus, nobody wants to be around someone too serious and critical all the time. Making other people laugh, especially our partner, allows us to take attention away from ourselves and our concerns. As you laugh with your husband or wife, you lessen the chances of feeling depressed. Small problems that were once magnified can be taken lightly and you can be offered a wider perspective on life. Exchanging jokes and lighthearted humor eases the burden of life, while supplying your relationship with more strength and joy.

The success of our relationships are not a one-time effort. Because relationship is the most important decision you'll make, every good-natured joke we share with our spouse means more than laughing. It means a more pleasant home, a more romantic relationship where there is less criticizing and more wonderful times shared. Always find ways to make each other laugh. You will reap the benefits of a joyous life with your partner and have a heart big enough to embrace your partner, flaws and all.

Tip 7: Be willing to Compromise

"Compromise is what binds people together. Compromise is sharing and conciliatory, it is loving and kind and unselfish."
— Ali Harris, The First Last Kiss

Compromise is vital in any relationship. Compromise is the building block that makes two different people a single unit - a team. When you were single, it was probably real easy to do what you wanted, when you wanted. You had full control of every decision in life, such as where to live and what to have for dinner. In a serious relationship, you have the responsibility to let another person in on the decision-making. You both should get equal amount of say, both on the big issues and the little ones.

Many couples negate compromising, assuming life is too short to settle a dispute by mutual concession. Some even say that committed relationships remind them of childhood, as they have to get someone's approval on many things. Truth be told, compromise is integral in healthy relationships. At the time you vowed to love each other and be in a serious relationship, you ought to have known that you won't be getting your way a hundred percent of the time. You're part of a team now and it's not just about you.

Anyone who disagrees on compromising might say, "Yes,

compromise is a good thing but every relationship is different. My partner and I are happy taking turns. We don't bother mastering the art of compromise." While it's true that every relationship is different, one thing's for sure: happiness is a team effort. It's not going to be a blissful union if one person becomes the doormat while the other one always gets their way. As a team, you should learn to be supportive of each other, to listen while your other half shares their thoughts and feelings. Put the other person first when possible and healthy to do so, without of course sacrificing your dignity and self-respect.

Here are ideas to help you compromise better:

1. **Remember it's not just about your way or their way.** Think of a few ways you can include your partner in working toward individual concerns. Combine your desires with theirs. Compromise doesn't only mean "a way of reaching an agreement in which each person or group gives up something that was wanted in order to end an argument or dispute." Maybe in business, but not in a personal and intimate relationship. It's not just about keeping the waters calm. Compromise also means combining the qualities of two different things. An example of a typical situation is if your loved one says they want to move to another city but you're not too keen on their choice. One good approach

is to stay in a spot where neither of you feels like you're sacrificing personal desires for the other person entirely.

2. **Let your better half express their point of view.** In any healthy relationship, it does wonders when two people can express concerns and expectations effectively. Let your partner know your stand on things, such as how you would like to deal with relatives and how money is spent. Lay expectations on the table. When your other half tells you what they want, always listen attentively.

3. **Agree on little things.** It can come as a surprise for plenty of people how the little things can become so important in a committed relationship. You've heard of the quote "don't sweat the small stuff". If the little things - such as where to shop for groceries, who takes out the trash tonight, or how loud is too loud when music is played - isn't addressed, the little things are sure to increasingly irritate each of you and small chagrins become big issues.

4. **Remember that compromise is teamwork.** It's a given that if we're on a team, we ought to deal with other people's preferences, no matter how much we want to insist on our own way. In a relationship, it's normal to have one person, in varying times, who needs more support and the other one who's in a place to give more. It's a cycle.

Nobody should be on top all the time.

5. **Discuss problems calmly.** When it comes to conflicts in intimate relationships, people usually firmly stand their ground until they get their way, or they passively back down to give in to their partner's wishes. When someone is exasperated, they tend to give up in a power struggle. Resentments can build up from this. Fighting fair is key. Make an effort to communicate with your loved one without raising your voice. Take a short break - enough for a pleasant walk or a few episodes of your favorite TV show - and tackle the problem once more when you're both more calm.

6. **Work together to find a middle ground.** Compromising is about meeting each other halfway, with love as the underlying current - not to simply keep the boat from rocking, or to shut your loved one up. Besides, how will you get along well with your partner when you don't have a middle ground? When we truly care for someone, we should find a way to at least meet them halfway, especially if the other person has different reasonable needs. When you started dating, you were able to build a romantic bond because you had things in common. You wouldn't get to the point of a committed relationship unless there's something that's keeping you connected. Finding a middle ground involves talking

about contradictory opinions in a respectful manner, then deciding together that one choice or the other is the best course of action.

You and your mate will encounter major conflicts at some point in your relationship. Conflicts occur because of our desires to be right. Remember that you're both working towards a mutual goal - a happy and intimate life together. Will you fight for what you think is your due, or passively surrender to your partner's demands? If you think both choices won't help in saving your relationship, consider one more option - compromise.

Tip 8: Be Willing to Forgive

Forgiveness is a sign that the person who has wronged you means more to you than the wrong they have dealt.
-Ben Greenhalgh

"In sickness and in health, 'till death do us part" - very familiar lines that we've often heard. The same goes for "I love you. I won't ever hurt you." and "You're the only one for me." These words shouldn't be uttered as cliches. At least, that's the whole point of commitment. Glance at the steep divorce rates and it's easy to be convinced these promises are often broken. Promising your faithfulness and love to another person means opening a whole life to them. The recipient of these and other similar promises breaks down walls of emotional protection in order to accept the words, baring their own soul. People build walls around themselves their whole lives and the moment a committed relationship is entered into, these walls are broken down as another person is welcomed to enter. What happens when the person who was supposed to protect you and be there for you through thick and thin is the very person who betrays and inflicts deep pain? How do you recover, let alone rise, from such searing pain? Are you going to build the wall right back up, or remember your own vows of "forever"?

The truth is, anyone is vulnerable to deep pain in an intimate and serious relationship. This person promised to love you, only you, and be there for you in ways even your own best friends and family won't. You freely allowed another person to enter your life. In all long-term relationships, there will come a time when your partner will cause you pain and suffering. Big or small, intentional or not, it's important you remember that the moment you entered that covenant to be in a committed intimate partnership, you were ready to have a heart big enough to understand the imperfections of your mate. You are supposed to guide one another along a journey called life. Forgiveness doesn't mean closing your eyes and pretending the offense didn't taken place.

Being the offended party is not an easy role to play, but you can't allow your emotion to control the situation. Yes, by all means allow yourself to be angry and feel pain. This is part of the process, and an instrumental one at that, if you're to get over the hurt. The key thing to remember is the place of hurt isn't a state that's meant to be permanent. Finding strength to forgive requires plenty of strength to muster, but it's very important you raise yourself to the occasion. After you've allowed yourself to grieve, find a time to get a good grasp of your emotions in order to handle the situation more logically. You might be seeing just one side of the story, which can keep you from moving on and not able to analyze the whole picture with a clearer view. There are times, after all, where you will feel offended due to a weaknesses in your loved one's fundamental trait, something that is not to be taken personally. Perhaps she has always been a type A personality and her career has been number one, way before she met you. Or maybe he has always been terrible at remembering dates and is prone to yelling when he feels frustrated. In these cases, you need to understand that these weaknesses are the real enemy and the solution is not to attack the offender - your loved one. You can sit down and discuss as a team how you can cope with the weaknesses and, maybe, eventually turn them into strengths.

It's easy talking about forgiveness when small mistakes are involved, but what if the issue is unfaithfulness? How can you begin to find the strength to forgive and move on? This is a very tough call. By all means, be angry, sad, resentful, even hateful. Allow yourself to feel the strong emotions that will naturally come about from your partner's massive betrayal. Do keep in mind to not act out on very intense emotions. Take time off away if you want to, and if you're able to. Allow yourself to take a break and surround yourself with friends. Keep yourself busy doing what you love. These are all normal and healthy ways to cope. Of course, you can't run forever. Broken trust is very difficult to restore. Remind yourself you're not the only one, nor will you be the last, to go through such pain. It will take strength - both emotional and physical - to be able to rise again. It will help to remember that we have all been recipients of forgiveness. We all have committed errors, grave and small, unknowingly and deliberately, yet we were allowed to move on. Being the recipient of this bitter favor, we now are accountable to give forgiveness a chance. Painful it may be, but to forgive is very essential to keeping the relationship. A serious relationship is not just another game, one where when you're offended, you just say "Okay that's it, I quit." A commitment to love involves a commitment to forgive. I don't mean to say anyone should stay in an abusive relationship. When addictions, mental illnesses, or plain old cruelty is involved, leave and seek help immediately. I'm talking about otherwise healthy relationships between reasonable adults that have fallen prey to the erring ways of man. Holding on to resentment rots the spirit, derailing us from a life that's meant to be filled with peace, growth and fulfillment. Forgiveness closes and seals holes in our relationships created by offenses that could potentially destroy the whole thing. As you forgive, do it with sincerity, and do not be afraid to trust again. Gather yourself, wipe away the dirt, move on as best as you can while accepting that pain is a normal part of the journey, and face the day as though it's breaking of a new dawn. We may not see it today, but as we forgive and move on in what was once a relationship full of promises, we're helping and strengthening our partner, making them eager to fix things in life, and making them realize once again that you're partners and there's no such thing as an offender or enemy between the two of you, if you're both committed together.

How you overcome a painful situation is going to be another level of courage required of you and your partner. Often times, situations needing forgiveness are make or break moments in your relationship. It's always going to be the choices you make during these circumstances that require you to forgive a repentant mate that will decide where your union goes. You may choose to face it with tears and decide you deserve better and start anew, or choose to rise up after that fall and use that occasion as another level up for you and your partner. After all, just like in life, it's not simply about how either one of you has fallen, but how you managed to rise up together.

Tip 9: Keep the Fire of Romance Alive

"Love looks not with the eyes, but with the mind, And therefore is winged Cupid painted blind."
- William Shakespeare, *A Midsummer Night's Dream*

We all know the jokes. Once you're committed to a long-term relationship, passion tapers off like a comedian who has lost the attention of the crowd after doing the same repetitive routine night after night. The verve, the playfulness, and the anticipation. It's a fact that repetition dulls the mind and even the most passionate couple can slip into ruts and find themselves wondering where the fire went.

How do we keep that fire alive, that je ne sais quoi? The cheap and easy answer is to look outside for blame and outside for answers. Workload, kids, stress, and exhaustion are all external problems that can be addressed with internal answers. A strong relationship looks within itself for the answers to challenges that arise; even how to keep the romance alive.

Bring Back the Play

Love and passion begin with playful flirting. You don't just up and get married, you flirt and date first. So if you find yourself in a rut bring in a little humor and playfulness. A simple, innocent, and eloquent solution to monotony. A light moment removes tension, relieves stress, and opens up avenues to spontaneous passion. A reminder of that first spark can kindle the fire gone dormant.

Re-visiting a familiar and old date spot and a teasing reminder of an old inside joke can bring out feelings and emotions in an earnest way, a way that circumvents and, sometimes, even exceeds the grand romantic gesture.

Set Appreciation Booby Traps

If you want to show you care you pay attention to the details. The off-hand comments that are oft-forgotten can be a trigger for a strong positive reaction. No one can remember every little thing, but if you plug a reminder in your phone for something mentioned in passing - an event or maybe a sale - you can surprise your partner and create passionate feelings at later dates.

These appreciation 'booby traps' can be as simple as putting a favorite tie or dress, one your partner mentioned you look nice in, and putting it in your weekly rotation. Now you have a subtle weekly reminder that you care about what your partner thinks of your appearance. A sentimental or favorite picture taken from an old box and slipped into your wallet or purse will, inevitably, be found one day by your partner. The significance of you carrying something with you that's so important to them, and the fact they discovered it themselves, will build a surge of positive feelings in your partner - kindling romance faster than a candle lit dinner and in an everyday, normal way.

Make Time Together on a Regular Basis

Taking time as a couple to plan some alone time together every week can be a huge avenue to romance. Nothing opulent, nothing overdone, just a simple time together where you can be honest and alone, without distractions. Not only does this allow you time to improve your relationship together, it gives you both something to look forward to. Allow a shared anticipation to bring a little excitement to your relationship. Sometimes it may be difficult to squeeze the time out of an already wrung-out schedule, but creating a regular time to just be the version of yourselves when you first got married can revive the honeymoon passion.

Listen

There are some huge misconceptions about listening in relationships. First and foremost is the idea that one gender is better than the other at listening, or that being older and wiser means you are a better listener. Neither of these perceptions are accurate. Listening is a skill that's easy to actively improve on every day.

Listening also goes beyond just hearing information and filing it away mentally. Good listeners pay attention to the ideas behind the words, the emotions and feelings behind the tone. Actively opening yourself to empathizing to what your partner is communicating, verbally and non-verbally, will sharpen your senses. You will begin to pick up on and notice minutia. These fine details will allow you to reciprocate and help build your partner up. The little signs of extra effort are what make a strong relationship enduring, and what keeps the romance burning. We all want to know we're understood, safe, and appreciated.

Change Something Up

Variety is the spice of life. An old saying, but a true one. Stuck in a rut? Put a little spice on it. Dress yourself up, change your hair style, add a new step to your routine. These are all subtle signals you can send to your mate that you still care about spicing things up, and these are signals that they'll often reciprocate. Feeling new and attractive in little ways will be reflected in your partner in only the way that a committed couple can reflect on each other. By putting a little shine back on the surface you can make a serious relationship that has maybe become a bit dull in the daily grind look polished and new, bringing the old passion roaring back to the center stage.

Keeping the romance alive shouldn't feel like a chore for a committed couple. Awkward feelings or exhausted resignation are the death of passion and can be combated with playful flirting, active listening, a small change here or there, and a thoughtful sign of appreciation delivered without pomp or ceremony.

Improving your relationship goes beyond conflicts and scheduling; it can be as straightforward as the simple, extra effort put into keeping the spark of romance vivid and alive.

Tip 10: Take Time for You: You are the most important person

"Be who you are and say what you feel, because those who mind don't matter, and those who matter don't mind."
— Bernard M. Baruch

Spending quality time with your partner is mandatory in keeping your relationship strong, exciting and continually growing in the right direction. Many individuals, however, tend to overdo it - or they're so consumed with the responsibilities of daily living - that they no longer have time for themselves. Missing out on alone time, or having a life outside your romantic relationship, can lead to strains that tug at your love life. This is most especially true when people curtail the personal growth and development of their partner, whether deliberately or unconsciously.

If you're in a committed relationship, it's normal to sometimes feel being tied up to your partner too tightly. This can be avoided and shouldn't be thought of as an inevitable outcome of your serious commitment to one another. Here are some ideas on how you can make your relationship healthier and more successful by allowing yourself to spend time with other people, or just enjoying some moments all by yourself.

1. **Plan a night out with friends.** When was the last time you actually hung out with your buddies or girlfriends and had a good time? If you can't even remember, then it's definitely time to pick up the phone or hit them up online for a wholesome group activity. Your lack of social life away from one another may be, unbeknownst to you in many cases, causing some of the tension between you and your mate. If you're partner is also the type who doesn't schedule time with their friends, encourage them and schedule your time away from each other on the same day. This way you don't go out to dine and have a great time with your pals while your partner feels rejected at home.

2. Enroll in a Class

Spending most of your free time doing the same times will get boring, even for individuals who love routine. Shake things up a bit by while learning something new or flexing your creative muscles by enrolling in a class. Join a class you've always wanted to join, or pick something new just for the sake of expanding your horizons. Join a group made up of beginner photography, if that's your thing. Sing up for a fitness class, an art class, or whatever can break the monotony in your life. The added bonus of enrolling in a class or joining a group of like-minded hobbyists is you not only get some healthy time away from your partner, you also add to your repertoire of knowledge and grow your social circle. Most people find a constantly improving person attractive and, chances are, you're partner will too.

    3. **Join a club.** Does your community have clubs you can join? Check out what clubs are offered near you and don't hesitate to sign up if there's one that catches your fancy. For instance, if you're an animal lover you can join a club composed of other individuals who have pets like you and be a part of their activities. There are also clubs that recruit members for volunteer work. Joining is your ticket toward a more rewarding life outside your relationship.

    4. **Start a new hobby.** Whether you're looking for ways to kill time or simply want to spend some time by yourself, starting a new hobby is a fantastic idea. Having a hobby has many benefits. To start, it can keep your mind off worries so you avoid getting stressed out. It also serves as an outlet for excess energy and creativity. Feel too drained from the rigors of your schedule? It's possible your energy drain might not simply be from physical exhaustion but from lack of inspiration. Many people find a hobby they love can relieve stress and even fight depression. You may even turn a hobby into an income generating project and earn extra money.

5. **Travel solo or with friends.** Can you remember the good old days when you saw places or went on road trips with your friends? Or that time when you get to visit another state, or even country, all by yourself? You can relive those moments, especially in the Internet age where online price-comparison for travelers opens up the doors of the world for a wide array of budgets. Ask friends to go on a cruise with you, or check out the latest recreational parks in neighboring towns. If traveling solo is your kind of thing, talk to your partner about traveling separately for an agreed amount of time. Since you'll be gone alone, this is one of those issues that you should openly discuss with them, out of love and respect. It could be a simple visit to family in a different city, or an overdue trip to see a long-lost friend.

Promising someone you'll be there for them forever is a serious commitment but it doesn't mean you have to spend every waking moment together. It's vital for you to understand each other's needs, and this includes spending time with other people you trust, or to be alone connecting with yourself

Do remember that your partner as a person who also needs room to grow. If they're asking for time away from you, remember that just because they want to doesn't mean they don't want your company.

Respecting each other and the space the other needs is part and parcel of a healthy relationship. Reasonable time spent away from each other, either to be alone or with people you both trust, can get you to intensely appreciate each other more once you reunite to continue the path you promised to pave together.

Tip 11: Relationships are Constant Practice

"For the things we have to learn before we can do them, we learn by doing them."
— Aristotle

It's hard to deny that we don't live in a culture where failure in relationships feels as though we're being smothered. Everywhere we turn we're hit in the face with failed relationships, be they ours or those of others. More so than in previous eras, we wear our shortcomings and previous experiences on our sleeve. Sometimes they become so much a part of us that we lose faith in our ability to have a lasting relationship. Admitting to having emotional 'baggage' is used commonly as a self-deprecating ice breaker, reinforcing the idea in our own mind in the shape of an everyday talking point.

The truth is we've become less forgiving of ourselves. We've lost the truth that, just like anything else, relationships take practice and failure. We first must acknowledge that our failures, our baggage, are just aspects of the journey to an enduring relationship. We cannot afford to lose faith in our ability to build a long-term relationship.

Culture of Failure

In part, it's not our fault that our confidence can be shaken after a number of stumbles. Now, more than any other time in the past, we are inundated with stories of failure - repetitive failure - as depicted in movies, songs, TV shows, and from friends and failures. The divorce rate is at an all-time high, which on one hand shows a willingness of people to move on from mistakes, it also is a shaping influence on our perception of relationships. The more of our friends and family members that divorce the more likely we are to presume it as a foregone conclusion.

The more our conscious mind is flooded with examples of failed relationships the more the idea can creep into our subconscious mind. It may be impossible to control the lives of those around us and what we see on TV, but we can actively work on our mental reaction to these stimuli. You can empathize with a friend going through a divorce without believing you are destined for the same thing.

Our culture shapes us, yes, but it does not completely define who we are. We always have the ability to mentally work on our own attitudes towards a culturally prescribed behavior.

Persistent Desire for Love

Yet, in spite of a cultural bombardment of failed relationships, the underlying message in all of the romantic movies and TV shows is the need for an enduring relationship; a lasting love. The idea of a soul mate and fairy tale ending is instilled into our minds at a very early age. Whether this construct is artificial in origin or not is beside the point, the fact is you want what you want regardless of the why's.

If you seek the fulfillment and stability of a lasting, committed relationship, then previous relationship mishaps and failures can wear you down. Eventually, your desire for that one relationship that transcends begins to feel more and more like a fairy tale. It becomes almost like a negative feedback loop; each failure feeding into the idea a successful relationship is possible and thus mentally moving you farther away from a point where you're prepared to build such a relationship.

Each new relationship begins to feel like a leap of faith. The thing about leaps of faith is that the more you take them, the more it feels like you're just punishing yourself.

Remind yourself that each new relationship is a clean slate. You're only bringing into it what you allow yourself to bring in from prior relationships. You have it in you to build the type of relationship that you want. It takes honesty and understanding with yourself and with your partner. But, to get to the starting point where you can build that relationship, you have to have confidence that you can reach your goal of a committed, happy relationship.

Self-Belief

Failed relationships slowly drain our confidence like an emptying gas tank. Eventually, we run out of fuel and just stall out on the side of the road. Too often, we're trapped into running on fumes pretending like the tank's filled to the brim.

If you want to half that self-belief, you first must fill up your tank. Confidence and self-belief affect self-esteem, how you go about your life, and how you interact with others. It will make you more attractive to yourself, and to others.

Learning to believe in yourself and in the possibility of a happy, enduring relationship begins with acknowledging your own failures and learning from them. In an environment where you're reminded of your own failures, constantly with parallels in media and popular culture, the importance of learning from your mistakes is underscored. Practice makes perfect, and your previous missteps are steps on the road to a happy relationship. Building confidence is a product of your mindset and attitude about your previous relationships - make your past relationships work for you and not against you.

Tip 12: Keep in Touch with Reality

"You know you're in love when you can't fall asleep because reality is finally better than your dreams."
— Dr. Seuss

When you have the confidence to begin building that long-term relationship your responsibility shifts from intensive self-monitoring regarding your own confidence to protecting the budding relationship.

Self-belief is important, vital even, to a successful relationship but it cannot override self-awareness. Always watch for warning signs, patterns that can be disruptive to your relationship. These patterns and these warning signs can come from yourself, from your partner, or from external sources. Confidence won't be enough to keep things on track when other influences threaten to derail your relationship.

Chronic Issues

The easiest way to predict future occurrences is by looking at the past. If a behavior or situation becomes a repetitive, chronic issue, it is important that you address the issue. The first thing to examine for chronic issues is within yourself. We have all our own history at our fingertips. With introspection and honesty, you can identify patterns in your own life that may present problems to a committed relationship.

Self-sabotage is one of the most destructive flavors of sabotage. We can do horrendous things to ourselves with the justification of self-preservation. It's a paradox and a trap that is easy to slip into. Sometimes the only way we can identify this chronic problem is through meticulous self-examination in a positive manner. We want to help ourselves out of a desire to improve and build, not to tear ourselves down for past mistakes.

The second place to examine for chronic issues is in your environment. This can include places such as at work; are there patterns at work that cause disruption in your personal life? Another example is family, is an over-bearing parent actively or passively disrupting your relationship? Once you can see the patterns in your life that bear influence on your relationship, you can spot the chronic interference that may lead to a relationship getting side-tracked. These are often subtle and hard to identify, but also major disruptions in which you're completely blameless.

Finally, keep an eye out for chronic issues in your partner. This is an area to tread lightly. It's very difficult to be in a relationship with someone who watches you with the keenness of a predator waiting to pounce. You don't want to create pressure or unease. But, it's important to watch for warning signs. If you can spot potential signs of problems, you can work to resolve them in a positive manner before they become problems. This is true for your partner and for yourself.

Warning Signs

Warning signs themselves can be a tricky area of business. What is a minor, passing inconvenience and what is indicative of larger issues? How do you know what is a legitimate warning sign and what is something that you should just shrug off?

The first easy way to tell if something is a red flag is the time test. Ask yourself if this was a problem last week or yesterday? If it's unresolved, will it be a problem tomorrow? In a week? In a year? If you find yourself answering yes to these questions, it's probably a warning sign and indicative of a potential roadblock.

Struggles with addiction - and not all addictions are to drugs - are a prime example of a warning sign that can persist and endure until it destroys a relationship. Financial issues will, sooner or later, influence a relationship. Debt, uncontrolled spending, and differing attitudes about financial planning are major warning signs for a successful, long-term relationship. Even inappropriate friendships can become a warning sign.

Actual or perceived issues in one partner's friendship can be an incredibly delicate but important issue to address.

There are many kinds of warning signs, knowing those that are threatening to the well-being of your relationship is something you need to acknowledge and identify, be they problems from yourself or your partner.

Checks and Balances

The solution is to install checks and balances. You want to build constructive and healthy boundaries to curtail behaviors or issues that are major warning signs or threats to your relationship. For example, if one partner has an unhealthy addiction to video games, the couple should set up healthy boundaries. A limit to the number of hours parked in front of a computer or TV playing games, or a set of tasks to be finished before the games come out.

These checks and balances are powerful stabilizing forces on our relationships. If partners work together to build constructive boundaries to destructive behaviors, the relationship becomes strengthened rather than undermined.

There is a key to building checks and balances. Healthy boundaries are boundaries that do not restrict but rather protect the good aspects of a relationship. The idea of building boundaries on negative behaviors is not to limit something your partner dislikes about you, but rather to protect the aspects of your character that your partner loves. If a boundary or check and balance system feels restrictive, it becomes easy to resent, and silent resentment is the assassin of a long term relationship. Build constructive boundaries that are healthy influences.

The goal of keeping an eye out for warning signs and chronic issues is to ensure that you keep in touch with reality while embracing your ability to build lasting love. Confidence is healthy but over-confidence is blinding. When you walk into a relationship, one you want to build for the long haul, do enter with open eyes. Only through honest observation can you spot the issues before they become problems, and build your relationship in a strong and enduring fashion to last for years into the future.

Tip 13: Establish a Bond

"Words are a pretext. It is the inner bond that draws one person to another, not words."
— Rumi

Part of being in a relationship is sharing an emotional connection. Things like pet names, small kisses on the forehead, snuggling, and intimate rituals. Are you feeling uncomfortable? A little squirmy? One does not have to be a helpless romantic in order to build that connection. Pet names and small signs of affection are not exclusive to the breaks between high school classes.

We build trust and emotional connections through affection. It's an integral part of being in a relationship. It doesn't matter if you're a steely pragmatist or a hopeless romantic, when you're in a committed relationship you need to build a bond with your partner. A healthy emotional connection is a foundation to an enduring relationship.

Showing Affection

Affection does not need to be grand romantic gestures nor does it have to be public. It doesn't matter if you want the world to see, or if you want to keep your affection behind closed doors. The important thing is to show affection. Affection is being vulnerable and showing trust. You're putting forth a small piece of you in an almost ritualistic fashion in order to get a response from your partner. This offering is a way of showing that someone is special or important, as this is not standard public behavior.

In the course of our life, shows of affection usually begin as a newborn with our parents. It's an integral part of early family life, be it with family or caretakers, and is a natural developmental cog for children. As it's so important to us as small children, it's little surprise that it's an intimate and bonding experience as our family and caretakers are the first other humans we bond with in life. By showing affection to your partner you demonstrate, truly actively demonstrate, that their importance equals that of the most important people in your life.

Being Uncomfortable with Affection

All of that being said, it's not uncommon - in fact, it's normal - to feel awkward and uncomfortable with overt shows of affection, especially in the beginning. That feeling of affectionate sluggishness is the origin of all the first-kiss angst usually associated with teenagers. But, it's a real thing. It takes time and active effort to build a comfort zone to where signs of affection are an everyday thing.

The level of discomfort varies with every person and it's important to be sensitive to your partner. Some people are less comfortable with overt public displays of affection and may react strongly to a kiss on the forehead. As with most aspects of a relationship, you need to build awareness and an open environment to feel these things out with your partner.

Affection is a two way street and if you take a turn off into a one-way alley you'll often find it leading to something more harmful than good.

Finally, being uncomfortable is one of the most transient feelings that exists. If someone is obviously feeling uncomfortable that feeling will spread faster than a cold. An awkward silence following an unexpected display of affection is a silence filled with doubts. If you find yourself in this position, open up about the situation and break the silence. A small joke is always a great way of easing tension and paving the way for a constructive conversation rather than snap, 'I hate it when you do that.'

Build Emotional Resonance

One of the problems with every day affection is that often times it feels cheap and doesn't resonate emotionally. A peck on the cheek out the door; does that really resonate as a show of love? A long-winded status update on Facebook may appeal to some but repulse others. How can you find a show of affection that resonates with your partner?

The answer is to try different types of affection and see what resonates with your partner. Simple trial and error. Some will be easy to figure out. If your partner loves surprises then giving small gifts at unexpected times is a wonderful way to show affection. If your partner is a really empathetic soul, sharing stories about your life and finding ways to let them connect with who you are and where you come from will strengthen your emotional bond. For the steely pragmatist, finding small ways of doing helpful things - such as household chores - when they don't ask will endear you to them.

Building emotional resonance is about finding the way to show affection that is best appreciated by your partner and then emphasizing it. Gently. Not only is it a sign of trust and intimacy, but it's a show of your knowledge of their personality. Your shows of affection become shows of love and recognition of character, and that is what resonates.

We do not get into relationships to maintain our bubble of personal space and perfect isolation. Part of building a connection with someone is building a bond of affection. It's an affirmation of trust. You are volunteering vulnerability in exchange for emotional fulfillment.

This is the core of building an enduring bond with someone.

Tip 14: Pick Your Battles Wisely & Fight Fairly

"He who cannot put his thoughts on ice should not enter into the heat of dispute."
— Friedrich Nietzsche, *Human, All Too Human*

During the course of a serious relationship, it's inevitable that disagreement and even open conflict will arise. Adults are deeply grained, complex people with decades of emotional history. So when conflict does occur, it's important to recognize what is important, what battles you should choose to fight, to help resolve the issue and strengthen your bond. In a committed relationship, you and your partner can't settle for the classic options of 'fight or flight,' you need to find that third option when you choose your battles, one that will help improve your union.

Is it important?

The first part of deciding if a conflict is worth pursuing, worth potentially opening up new or old avenues of emotional pain, is the time test. The time test is asking yourself "Will this matter tomorrow? In a week? Next year?" By stepping back from an emotional flash point and finding some perspective you can measure the import and impact of the conflict.

In the moment, with emotions flaring, it can be difficult to see something as silly and frivolous. But sometimes, you have to admit to yourselves that maybe something is not, in truth, as important as it feels in the moment. The time test is a good way to feel this out. Your partner forgetting to do the laundry may matter a little tomorrow, but probably not in a week and definitely not in a year. Maybe not worth a full volume argument. Yet, if that lack of laundry activity is a pattern over an extended period of time, then it's a safe bet it will still matter in a year of their still not doing laundry. The time test. It's a tactic to give yourself perspective before engaging in an emotional conflict.

Get to the Heart of the Matter

Conflict is often a difference in expectations. When expectations are not met or are felt to be excessive, conflicts bubble up to the surface. Another important key to finding perspective to determine if a conflict is worth escalating is to put yourself in the shoes of your significant other. Identify where the difference in expectations are, and when exactly expectations were not met. It's a vulnerable feeling when your mate, your partner in life, doesn't meet an expectation. We expect to be safe and understood in a serious relationship.

When an expectation isn't met, we feel unsafe and unsure of

ourselves. Take a moment to identify why your partner doesn't feel safe, determine where the real conflict lies. This has a two-fold purpose. We can identify why the conflict is happening, which allows us to decide if it's important enough to pursue, or to let slide. Also, it enables us to begin the rebuilding process to re-establish the safe and secure feelings.

Don't Pull the 'Trigger'

During the course of a courtship and relationship, there are very few sensitive emotional triggers that aren't pulled at one point or another. Over time, these triggers become apparent. When emotions are high, it's easy to try to gain an advantage by pulling out an old sore spot and just tapping lightly. Yet, when these triggers are known by both parties, pulling one doesn't really give you an advantage. It's a cheap tactic intended solely to hurt for personal gain and hurts twice as much for that recognition.

There's no need to fight dirty. Ideally, you're working to resolve a conflict, not to bring up known emotional triggers. Pulling one of these triggers undermines any effort to resolve the conflict, it undermines your mate's trust in you about their vulnerabilities, and takes what might be a minor conflict and escalates it to something major and hurtful. Instead of pulling an emotional trigger, try to find an emotional defusing point. A small joke or reminder of something joyful can take an edge off the tension and allow other emotions to help balance the conflict.

Build, Don't Battle

If we're forced to choose our battles, maybe we can change our approach to the battle. Battles are not good in a committed union. Instead of thinking of a conflict as a battle to be waged, instead try to think of it as an opportunity to build. A conflict in your relationship can tear down that safe feeling, and can tear through feelings. Instead of tearing things down in a battle, why not try building?

Perspective, empathy, and patience can help you build a stronger bond. When a conflict happens, try to focus on fixing the hurt of an unmet expectation. Figure out ways you can ensure that both your partner's and your expectations can be met in the future.

Sometimes a fight can be like breaking a bone. It hurts a lot when the break happens and there will be a rigid and awkward period while the break heals. But, when all is said and done, the bone is stronger than it was before.

Ultimately, choosing your battles means fighting a losing war simply because if you're fighting a war with your loved one, you've already lost. Looking at a relationship through the eyes of a military commander analyzing a campaign of war is a sure-fire sign of a relationship that's inevitably circling the proverbial drain.

Tip 15: Define what Love Means to Your Partner

"The consciousness of loving and being loved brings a warmth and richness to life that nothing else can bring."
—Oscar Wilde

Understanding what love means to your partner is one of the vital aspects of a successful relationship. But, perhaps that's one of the check boxes en route to promising forever. What about when you've been together for a long time already and you think you've already got their road map to love? Sometimes long-term relationships can lead us into a trap of complacency. Feeling safe and secure is different from being complacent. Routine and normality can be a welcome feeling, but understanding what love means to your partner means understanding that how your mate perceives and wants to feel loved can change. Strong relationships allow room for growth, but that room for growth needs to incorporate the growth of new perceptions and new needs when it comes to feeling loved.

Don't Slip Out of the 'Know'

People change with time, even your long-term mate. When there's a little wiggle room for growth, it's a good indicator. But, sometimes, wiggle room just doesn't cut it. Part of allowing for change is to know that sometimes preferences and needs require change as well. Stagnation is a crippling blow for any relationship. If we fall out of the 'know' about our partner's preferences and needs, we may find ourselves on the wrong side of growth—a growing gulf of distance between loved ones. A gulf of stagnation can swallow up a relationship with silent cruelty. Indifference, unchecked, will be the death of love.

Allowing for change goes beyond accepting new hobbies and social activities. It's opening yourself to being excited for who your partner could still become. We want to feel safe and secure in our relationships but it's impossible to control everything. There will inevitably be a little mystery about where you're going as a couple, and who you will continue to grow into. The strongest unions encourage growth and change, always learning about what it means to be loved.

Pay Attention to Complaints

Complaints, even small ones, are big sign posts to understanding what love means to your significant other. It takes a sacrifice to offer a complaint. You're offering up criticism, even constructive criticism, to someone you vowed to support and stand by. Complaints are not afterthoughts and they can teach us a lot.

A small complaint about not seeing enough of one another can indicate a growing need for quality time as a couple without distractions. A remark about not offering an arm or a hand as you walk through a mall can indicate a greater need for physical contact. Frustration over mixed words with children from parents can signal that your other half is feeling a need for greater positive support in your relationship.

It's easy to shrug off complaints as everyday occurrences of minor importance. But, there is almost always a subtext to a small complaint. With a little more thought and a little more empathy we can spot underlying shifts in needs and preferences. We can identify the ways our partner wants to be loved. The ways they want to be loved won't remain the same old story, just as your relationship isn't a single love story.

Questions to Ask Yourself

There are questions we can ask ourselves to identify if we are indeed out of sync with how our partner wants to be loved. Often enough, we simply have lost a bit of our listening skills - listening skills that connect on an emotional level. Ask yourself when was the last time you honestly asked for your mate's opinion on something. An opinion, or feelings on a topic, are a good way of spotting whether or not you're in sync. When was the last time you asked your partner to explain something to you? If you haven't let them explain a passion of theirs to you, maybe you've slipped out of the know. How about the last time you noticed something new about your partner, or some new behavior, that you really liked? It's easy to spot things we don't like but seeing something new that you like in your partner is a good way to ensure that you can continue to offer love in the ways they want.

Ask yourselves these questions and help gauge your how in tune you are with your loved one. A gentle question can lead to insights that show you the path to a minor course correction in your relationship. A small change now, an acceptance of the new and unknown, may put you on the path unknown, but save your relationship from a well-known, and inevitable, finish.

When we analyze our own interpretation of our partner's behaviors and emotions we open up our own avenues to love. We can continue to offer love and support in new ways. Committed relationships are as organic as any other living thing, they will grow and send new branches out in unexpected directions. Use your intuition to feel out subtle changes in the subtext of your relationship. Allow these changes to move you like a tide or a current. Attention to growth can slowly move your bond into new directions you didn't anticipate—and be all the better for it.

Tip 16: Make Peace with the Fact that You Can't Control Everything

"You can not always control circumstances, but you can control your own thoughts."
~Charles Popplestone

Part of embracing another human being in a committed relationship is accepting vulnerability. Your exposing your heart and emotions to great risk. Being in a relationship means investing a significant part of your emotional well-being into another person, a person who you'll ultimately have no control over. You can never completely control the actions of another person. The heart is often portrayed as hidden in a castle protected by emotional walls that need to be breached and great iron gates that need to be opened. In fact, the heart is a piece of yourself that you offer for the promise of greater emotional gain. In this way, it's a gift with the expectation of reciprocation.

Reciprocation is so deeply ingrained in human nature that we are pre-conditioned to reciprocate a gift. It's been proven repeatedly the positive impact of bringing coffee to your boss when you intend to ask for a raise. A subconscious need to reciprocate immediately presents itself in the boss' mind. Of course, an overhanded offering like a new car will result in an overt realization of the expectation of reciprocation, and surely will backfire. Never take a sledgehammer into surgery. But, an earnest and simple gesture activates the reciprocation effect.

The human *need* to reciprocate pre-exists. But, in a relationship you're offering your heart—your emotional well-being. A far greater offering and a far greater risk than a latte.

The risk is we can't control everything, we can't control someone else's response to this offering. Anytime something is risked, there is a fear of that risk coming back to bite us. When it's our hearts, this fear can overwhelm us. Sometimes, the fear of unrequited love can lead to a perfectly successful and rational person sabotaging a relationship. Fear of unrequited love can cause someone else to never put their heart out there, to behave as if their heart is indeed a treasure locked in a forbidden castle.

The feeling of locking your heart in a castle gives an illusion of control. By sealing up ourselves, we create a mirage of security. But, the truth is that the idea of a castle awaiting a hero or champion to break through is a fallacy. The castle is empty, there is no laughter in the halls. That empty feeling will spread throughout you and your life until you lose any control at all over your own emotions and feelings. The world becomes filled with fear and mistrust of those moving around us, we become so obsessed with our own safeguards.

The fear is born out of lack of control. We have to accept that we cannot control everything. We cannot control our partner, or our relationship. The only control we really have is the decision to put ourselves out there, or to remain feeling empty inside our hearts' well-warded castle. So how then do we handle the total lack of control we have with regards to matters of the heart?

The answer is to embrace the fact we have no control. You will have zero control over your relationship, until you embrace the fact that you have no control. By admitting we don't have control over everything we acknowledge our fear that we can get hurt.

When we admit we have no control, we allow gain a new kind of control.

Love can feel like a rip tide that flings us far from the beach out into the wide ocean. Suddenly, the beach is far away, we're moving without control, and we're at risk of drowning. You cannot swim against a rip tide, it's too strong, you have to accept that you have no control. Once you've accepted your lack of control, you relax and you can begin to swim parallel to the beach, moving yourself out of the rip tide by not moving against it. From there, you can easily swim back to safety.

It's in this way that we must embrace the fact that we cannot control everything in our relationship. When we find ourselves swimming against a strong current unexpectedly we'll drown if we try to fight it. There will always be the unexpected. If we accept the new and choose to move not in opposition but in a parallel direction, we retake control of our own life.

If we want to improve our relationship, we must surrender to the chaos that undermines the control and security we cling to. This is why if we want to improve the relationship, the solution is to pour more of yourself into the relationship. We can only do this if we accept the risk of ultimate rejection. We cannot control our partner's decisions, but by embracing the lack of that control, we can continue to offer, accept, and reciprocate love strengthening our relationship as time passes.

Tip 17: Draw Strength From Others

"Being deeply loved by someone gives you strength, while loving someone deeply gives you courage."
— Lao Tzu

A common trend I see in the fast-paced modern world is the isolation of one's personal life from one's friends and family. In a world of instant messaging and more apps that allow for remarkable communication, there's less exchange of truly meaningful emotional vulnerabilities. The 'LOL's' and 'hahas' have overrun humanity's greatest advantage: the ability to draw strength from others. The problem lays in misconceptions that have become popularized about accepting help and surrounding ourselves with others who also value commitment.

Accepting Shows Weakness

There are so many misconceptions about asking for and accepting help. Perhaps the greatest, is that it shows a lack of independence. There's a disconnect between the idea of being independent and the idea of having a support network. An individual can be independent, and is so when they enter a relationship, but that doesn't mean they cannot surround themselves with others to ask help for when needed. Too often we seek to make divisions and compartmentalize life.

We want to have a work life, a social life, and a personal life and allow for no overlap between the three.

The truth is that overlap is inevitable and it offers us a resource for far greater understanding and acceptance than we can find if divided. How can someone at work understand issues you're having in your social life if the two are completely separated, and vice versa? By allowing for overlap, we allow for a much wider circle of individuals we can turn to for support.

Another reason we often don't turn to others for support and help is that we're afraid. Afraid of rejection, afraid of vulnerability, and afraid to burden others with our problems. These fears feed into the idea that we're being weak or irresponsible by seeking help from those around us - be they family, friends, or co-workers.

People are not islands in the expanse of an open ocean. We are inundated with human contact non-stop every day. We're a communal species by nature. Allowing these fears to overwhelm us is the weakness. Not having the courage to offer up our problems for our friends and loved ones to help us.

Reciprocating Support Networks

Overcoming our fears and admitting that we need help are no

small matters. Asking someone for help with a personal issue is a sign of trust and value. It's a sacrifice to put a vulnerable foot forward in this situation, and as such, the person you turn to for support automatically feels obligated to offer the best and most helpful Tip they can. This is natural human reciprocation at work. By surrounding ourselves with people who share the same values and commitment to relationships, we're ensuring a cycle of reciprocation and support.

The strongest circles of friends are often built upon years of this reciprocated support. The emotional scrapes and bruises salved by the words and support of our friends and family leave an impact on us as surely as a negative experience leaves a scar. When we help others and turn to them for help, we fortify a community and support network. These networks are invaluable as they are breeding grounds for respect, honesty, loyalty, and kindness. An individual without the reservoir of these emotions and feelings becomes hardened, mistrustful, and cold. All three of these negative emotions will become triggers for an empty and unhappy life. In this way, a close circle of friends, allowing others to help us, is as much preventative as it is cathartic.

Asking for Help with Love

Yet, even the strongest support networks may seem intimidating to turn to when it comes to matters of the heart. Sometimes the pressures of culture or society can impose themselves even in these safe and welcome environments. A common instance is if someone in a relationship discovers that their partner is cheating on them. We already know what our friends will say: kick em' to the curb! But, sometimes we're not ready to sacrifice a relationship in this abrupt and permanent way. We have to do honest soul searching - a process that can be far less lonely and painful with someone to help us and support us.

The knee-jerk societal reaction of being strong and ending things immediately, however, prevents us from turning to our support network for help. We already know what answer they're going to give, and the reservations they'll keep just-below-the-surface if we don't immediately break things off. In some small way, they will judge us.

Ultimately, the answer is to find someone who'll offer Tip and support without judgments. Even if you fear the pressure of a cultural expectation, trust your friends, trust your family. They will surprise you. What you expect of others in a time of fear, betrayal, and loneliness will be biased towards the negative. There's a reason we invest so much in reciprocating support throughout a network of loved ones: so when the hard times come we have those we can explain our feelings to without fear.

Having someone to turn to when you're feeling the ultimate betrayal is the first step to healing. By turning to others for help, by building support networks of those who share our value of commitment, we are putting a down-payment on emotional well-being that will last a lifetime.

Tip 18: Relationships can land us anywhere: The goal is to stay together.

"Sometimes, reaching out and taking someone's hand is the beginning of a journey. At other times, it is allowing another to take yours."
— Vera Nazarian

We willingly enter a long-term romantic commitment with forever etched in our minds. The desire to grow old together is part of the dream when we exchanged vows with our partner, be they voiced out in a crowded church adorned with lovely flowers, or privately whispered promises echoing the same romantic pacts uttered by lovers who have come and gone before us. It is a rare individual who doesn't crave the dream of a forever love, one that will stand the test of time, the nuances of every day. A long life can be a lonely existence without a special someone by our sides, after all.

In your current relationship, how do you and your partner see to it that you'll be walking hand in hand through the decades? It has been said death and taxes are the only sure things in life. No matter how solemn the romantic assurances are, no matter how heartfelt the vows may be, there are no guarantees when it comes to intimate relationships and their lifespan. Fortunately, there are ways to ensure the increased success of your mutual goal of being together. One of these ways is working towards more specific goals together.

Setting Concrete Goals

While a happily ever after is indeed a shared dream between you and your significant other, it can be a bit vague, too broad. One of the keys is to have specific goals that you as a team work to achieve. This way you can both check and align yourselves against these definitive objectives. Are you spending as much time each week as you'd like? Setting a specific duration of the amount of time you want to invest in your relationship – a time that you and your other half mutually agree to – will help you both avoid the common mistake of being like two ships passing in the night. Saying "We should spend more time enjoying each other's company every week" is too generic, while agreeing on a specific day for a date night will land you towards more intimate moments. If the date night on Wednesday failed to materialize for whatever reason (work, the kids, etc.), you two will know a catching up is in order. If Friday night each week has been discussed to be the time to block out for your relationship to grow, then you can make the other priorities in life work around your relationship, as opposed to your schedule working you.

Brainstorming as a Team

In an intimate relationship, not all goals will be about your bond. Your partner will have their own ambitions – dreams related to career, children, spirituality, financial status and more. The happiness and fulfillment of each of you as individuals will have tremendous impact on your relationship. Knowing this, keep communication lines open and hear out your partner when they talk about their goals. Have a set guideline when you're both discussing aspirations in the near future. The guideline can include things like talking about short-term goals - "What do you want to achieve at work, at home, or in the relationship in the next three months? Six months? A year and five?" Brainstorm together specific steps that can be undertaken to get closer to any of your ambitions.

A great idea is to schedule a time, at least once a month, to discuss your goals – both individual and mutual – to find out how if you're on track and what can be done to support one another. A team effort does have its perks after all. While you have the duty to support your partner and have their happiness in mind, you can reap the wonderful token of having someone by your side who likewise should act as an emotional cornerstone to walk through life with you.

When talking about your goals as a couple and as individuals, be open to feedback. Your partner is more than a sounding board. Giving them an opportunity to help you meet goals by listening to their suggestions will show them how you appreciate your significant other and the talents and skills they bring into the conversation. This will also be a wonderful opportunity to thank your partner and compliment them on suggestions they offer that you can use to bring you both closer to your goals. When you engage in these intimate moments brainstorming about goals and checking progress, be sure to write notes down. If you find this notion a tad unromantic in the beginning, think of the notes as a journal, as opposed to rigid notes one would take at an office meeting. You can write both your names on the cover of the notebook. Studies time and time again have shown how goals written down on paper significantly come into fruition more than those merely held in our minds.

Goals as a Bonding Experience

If you and your partner find that specific goals you have in the near future involve individual goals instead of mutually shared dreams involving your relationship, use this as an opportunity to create mutual goals. While it's a given you both have the same goal of staying together, specific dreams to be achieved in the next six months (or less) will provide you intimate common grounds. It can be a goal of saving up for a vacation within a year, or a goal of volunteering a set number of hours at a non-profit you both support. Whatever it may be, make sure it's specific and is in line with shared values you both hold. This shared goal to be achieved in the next few months will provide more bonding opportunities for the both of you, while giving you concrete rungs on your relationship ladder, one that leads to a mutually satisfying life together.

Tip 19: Do unto your partner as you want him/her to do to you

"True love is not a hide and seek game: in true love, both lovers seek each other."
— Michael Bassey Johnson

Since we were small children, we were instructed to be nice kind to others. To treat others the way we want to be treated. While excellent Tip for small children, as adults we begin to identify discrepancies between being nice and being kind.

There is a marked difference between being nice and being kind. In relationships, it's far more important to be kind than to be nice. That's because the difference comes in sincerity. You can be nice without being sincere, but kindness is rooted in sincerity.

The Image Problems of Being 'Nice'

Being nice has some image problems. Being nice is sometimes associated with being fake or pretentious. The idea of someone who's always polite and nice on the surface, but is actually conniving and mean-spirited, has embedded itself into meaning of 'nice.' The meaning of nice has literally shifted in its usage in language over time. Nice can now mean multiple things and be for multiple purposes.

Often times being nice is a coping mechanism for dealing with difficult people. It's a passive way of circumventing directness or conflict. In some instances, this is a highly productive and successful tactic. In other cases, however, it can create even more tension as, when overtly done, it can feel condescending.

Another instance is when someone who's behaving excessively 'nice' is activating the imagery of a benevolent, if pretentious, authority figure behaving towards a subject. Nobody enjoys being treated this way but the ways in which someone is being 'nice' is still the same.

The meaning behind being nice has been tainted ever so slightly. At the very least, it can raise doubts and questions as to the sincerity of the behavior.

Doubts and questions are two words that reveal red flags when in the context of a relationship. When there is doubt, or when one party questions the sincerity of their partner, problems are sure to follow. Already the openness and honesty of the relationship is cast into doubt. Suddenly your footing is very unsteady. The many veiled meanings behind 'nice' behavior should remove it as a means of emotionally connecting with your partner.

Being Kind

Being kind, on the other hand, eliminates all questions as to sincerity. The semantics of kind have remained stoic and unchanging in their meaning. A kind person is one who is sincere. An act of kindness, by definition, bears a sincere aspect of forethought or generosity that's beneficial to the recipient alone. This is the key distinction between being nice and being kind. Someone who is nice can be self-serving at the same time. Someone who is being kind is only serving someone else.

When we put this distinction into the context of a relationship, it's easy to see why we want to be kind but not nice to our partner. Relationships work on the foundation of reciprocity and emotional fulfillment. The more you put in for your partner, the more you get out of the relationship. It's a down payment for your mutual happiness. If we view nice through the lens of being simultaneously self-serving, we understand why this fails and even undermines a relationship. Instead of putting your partner first, and allowing yourself to benefit second, you're trying to have your cake and eat it too. Serving your partner and yourself at the same time, with equal emphasis, robs the reciprocity and fulfillment structure of a relationship, robs it of its value. It's a shortcut, and shortcuts don't lead to enduring relationships.

Kindness doesn't condescend, it doesn't put on airs. It doesn't pretend to be something it's not. These are not just characteristics of kindness, they're characteristics of someone we want to share a relationship with - they're a model of behavior. If kindness represents sincerity, then it is an embodiment of the sentiment associated with a genuine and lasting relationship. You can be nice to someone in the supermarket, but true kindness is a far rarer interaction. Much like showing affection, showing kindness is an intimate experience that goes beyond the usual bubble of interaction we maintain between us and casual acquaintances.

At one point in the past, nice and kind may have been true synonyms. But, in modern days, there's a gap between the two in meaning, a gap that encodes a distinction that is of special relevance to relationships. As such, truly endeavor to treat your partner with kindness. Being kind is going beneath the surface to show true sincerity, while being nice is at the surface level and can leave ambiguity as to intentions.

Finding ways to be kind is finding ways to bond with your partner, strengthening your relationship as you move into the future together.

Tip 20: Be Sexually Liberal

"Marriage should be between a spouse and a spouse, not a gender and a gender."
— Hendrik Hertzberg

Just because you're in a long-term relationship doesn't mean the fire has to die and the passion must fade. Having good sex is just as important to the success of a relationship as being friends or having similar financial goals. A sexually unsatisfying relationship stagnates quickly and breeds 'What if' questions for wandering minds. Yet, sex is often one of the harder topics to be open about with your partner. By definition, it's a sensitive topic, and one that becomes more difficult to talk about the longer concerns go unvoiced.

Therefore, it's important to always be sexually generous. Just like many other facets of a relationship, sex operates on a basis of reciprocity between you and your partner; the more you put in the more you'll get out of sex in a healthy relationship.

Be Generous in Bed

Conflict and discontent arises out of differing expectations. In the context of a one-night stand, this isn't so important. Expectations will be different, but that won't matter as it's a once-off experience. Sometimes those differing expectations lead to new experiences which can be exciting. However, one-night stands, while exciting in the moment, feel empty afterwards. This is due in part to the fact that your expectations aren't met and nor are your partner's.

This is committed people with a healthy sex life don't envy their single friends. When you meet someone else's expectations, and they meet yours, the sexual experience is far more satisfying and fulfilling. Now, this is not exclusive to those in a committed relationship, but it is far more predictable and regular.

At the crux of this fulfilling sexual experience is the tenant of being generous. If you concern yourself with your partner's expectations first you're ensuring that they're having a good time. In business, if you want someone to do something for you, ensuring they're in a good state of mind is a great starting place. This is true between the sheets as well. You're activating their need to reciprocate and, in turn, they will strive to meet your expectations of an exciting and fulfilling sexual experience.

What if My Partner isn't Meeting My Expectations?

This can be an uncomfortable situation to be in – a partner who isn't meeting your sexual needs and expectations. It's a difficult topic to broach as you're dealing with two sexual experiences at the same time. The best course is to be open and gentle in discussing the topic. Honesty is absolutely necessary. A repressed need can easily slip into a repressed desire which engenders resentment and can ultimately lead to a search for another sexual partner.

Addressing the topic can be difficult. Be sensitive to your partner's feelings. Expressing a need in the bedroom is not just about you, it's about them too. They're an active participant. If one of your needs is something they're unwilling to fulfill, constructive compromise is needed - one that requires a very open conversation. The need is unlikely to disappear, especially if it's refused for whatever reason. Left alone, it will continue to seethe and grow within you. Hence, compromise becomes a powerful tool for ensuring that the sex is good for both of you. Also, a partner who is sexually satisfied is far more likely to try and fulfill your needs than one who is not. The best bargaining chip is often being sexually generous with your partner.

Addressing Change in the Bedroom

Finally, it's important to acknowledge that sexual needs and desires change over time, just like any other part of your relationship. It's important to be able to have honest conversations and leave room for growth in the bedroom. Sometimes the same old combination isn't going to unlock the experience you both want, especially as time moves on. It can be dangerous when sexual desires change but the expectations remain static and immobile.

Part of being sexually generous is being malleable to change. It's always possible your partner may want to try something different. Sex is supposed to be exciting and stimulating, a new experience may lead you to react in unanticipated ways. This is where being open and honest with your partner is important. If you branch out in bed, being able to talk afterwards about the experience, be it positive or negative, is vital. Allowing expectations to shift and change with your relationship will ensure that the sex is good and stays good.

It's crucial, however, to layout healthy borders with your partner to protect a good sexual experience. A new experience is not always good if it crosses a fundamental restriction that you or your partner has. This is why setting up healthy boundaries to protect the sensitivities of both you and your partner, and thereby protecting the sexual experience, ensures that changes and new experiences stay within the realm of pleasure for both of you.

Sowing generosity in the bedroom is a sure-fire way to ensure a positive sexual experience. The rewards of exciting, passionate sex where both partners' sexual needs are addressed and allowed to change are reaped. By being generous, you're putting the priority on sex together as a team, as opposed to what you alone get out of sex. Good sex is an important part of our vitality, and keeping a relationship viable for years to come.

Tip 21: Being Available When Needed is Always Important

"You can talk with someone for years, everyday, and still, it won't mean as much as what you can have when you sit in front of someone, not saying a word, yet you feel that person with your heart, you feel like you have known the person for forever.... connections are made with the heart, not the tongue."
— C. JoyBell C.

Availability is a cornerstone of the mutual agreement between two people entering a relationship. Being there and being present, emotionally and physically, is one of the fundamental human needs in a relationship. Life doesn't always afford us the opportunity to be both physically and emotionally there for our partner, but it's imperative to the survival of the relationship to be there for them as often as possible.

Physical contact is keenly important to humans, and physical support is critical to a relationship. But, strong and healthy relationships can survive times apart - sometimes even for extended duration. Being emotionally available, however, is absolutely crucial for the relationship to succeed and endure. When we're emotionally distraught, many times there are certain people we cannot turn to for one reason or another. But, in a relationship, we want to be able to rely on our partner, no matter what, to be emotionally available to us for support. We can't always predict when, where, why, or how our partner will be emotionally distraught, so it's important that we're emotionally available.

Being There Physically

For some, being there physically for support is just as important as being there emotionally. Physical support can mean many different things to different people. Sometimes being able to unwind with sex after a stressful day is what your partner needs, but it's just as likely as simply wanting to be held. Sometimes physical support means being there with them during a confrontation with a friend or family. Emotional support can be tied to physical support - by being present physically you're expressing emotional support.

Physical support, however, mandates being sensitive to what your partner wants. Much like showing affection and understanding how your partner wants to be loved, physical support needs to be carefully weighed and measured to give your partner what they need.

Being There Emotionally

Being there emotionally for your partner is one of the most important responsibilities you have in a relationship. It's an all-encompassing responsibility. It includes the day-to-day emotional support, as well as the emotional support during times of special difficulty. It requires a heavy investment of time and attention to another person, something which may not come naturally to everyone. Emotional support requires emotional investment. Being ready to invest emotional energy into another person is a prerequisite for a committed relationship. A relationship where one person does not feel emotionally supported is twice as taxing and becomes increasingly more emotionally burdensome as time passes.

This is why being in a long-term relationship requires both partners to be sensitive to the emotional state of the other. If you feel as though you aren't getting enough emotional support, it's difficult to bring it up. Admitting to feeling unsupported can be hurtful to both you and your partner, but it is the first step to receiving the support you need. Disclosing hurt feelings in a gentle manner – and listening to your emotionally injured partner - is also a cornerstone of a successful relationship.

The Danger of Being Absent

A lot of people think the most hurtful thing someone can do is to scream, yell, and fight with their partner. This isn't true. Anger and rage at least demonstrate passion. The most painful feeling is feeling dismissed, ignored – a partner who's indifferent to your existence, one who's emotionally missing in action. We commit to a relationship and invest a lot of ourselves emotionally. Feeling dismissed or ignored is unnerving, dangerous and damaging to the psyche. It leaves us feeling lost and unsure of ourselves. It can lead us into seeking more attention, to withdraw into a protective shell, or to lash out at those around us.

Feeling dismissed or ignored isn't just about the big things either. It can be as simple as an absent-minded "Uh-huh" when your partner's attention is clearly fastened on the TV. These small instances inflict an emotional toll on a painful account over time. As such, your responsibility is to be as attentive and sensitive to your partner's emotional well-being. Open and honest conversation about how your partner wants to be loved and supported are vital as your relationship grows and evolves over time.

A relationship, one that is going to endure and be healthy, mandates presence of being. Physical support, emotional support, and being there for your partner are parts of the comprehensive responsibilities of a healthy relationship. Investing in being there for your partner is infectious, and that support will be reciprocated when given time to grow and develop.

Tip 22: Be Grateful and Humble: It will take your relationship far

"Reflect upon your present blessings -- of which every man has many -- not on your past misfortunes, of which all men have some."
— Charles Dickens

Gratitude and perspective are two aspects of a relationship that can require a little time to take root and grow. But, given time to take hold, gratitude and perspective are two amazing tools during stressful times in a relationship. They allow us to take a step back and appreciate the emotional value of our partner at times when we need it the most.

Think of gratitude as a well you can tap to bring you refreshing water when you're parched for positive feelings. By taking time to be grateful for your relationship and your partner, you pour a little bit more into that reservoir of feelings you can access during any droughts at a later date.

The Power of Gratitude

None of us is perfect; in fact we're not even always perfect for one another. Fallacy is human and to be forgiven. This is why gratitude is so powerful. When you appreciate the little and the great things your partner does, you are preserving the wonderful things a relationship can grant. It gives you a lift in the moment, plus the ability to enable perspective at a later date during a difficult time.

In as much as the way you construct healthy boundaries to protect the good things in your relationship with your partner, with gratitude you preserve those good things so that they endure as your relationship continues. Gratitude in this way serves as a powerful emotional anchor. It's crucial that in a relationship where you invest so much energy, you have these anchors that stabilize you two, and stabilize the relationship when the water gets rough. This is the hidden power of gratitude: its stabilizing influence and nature. Life will always have peaks and valleys, doubly so with our emotions, but being grateful provides a constant mean for which you can rely on to pull you up when you feel down.

Showing Gratitude

The more overt power of gratitude is that overt displays of gratitude ingratiate your partner to you. A well-timed display of gratitude and affection, particularly in a stressful time, can evoke a strong positive reaction from your partner. It's an acknowledgement that proclaims, 'Even though I have flaws, and maybe my flaws are creating stress for my partner, I still appreciate everything that my partner does in this relationship.'

These reminders and admissions are what sustain someone during the difficult times. But, showing gratitude also has a day-to-day application. Displaying appreciation is a form of emotional support that demonstrates you are present and there for your partner. It's a selfless and kind act that shows earnest sincerity. Sincerity and kindness are salves to many sorts of hurt, especially those that are kept beneath the surface and may not be immediately noticed, if noticed at all. Simple gratitude goes beyond being nice or courteous – it's something that serves as a chronic reminder as to why you're together in the first place.

One of the best tips for showing gratitude is to move out of the usual medium of communication in your relationship. If you communicate primarily through text message or e-mail, try writing a letter to show gratitude. If you prefer talking on the phone or leaving notes for one another, try a digital-based expression of gratitude. By moving out of the norm, you emphasize and juxtapose the gratitude against the backdrop of the everyday.

Finally, and perhaps, the greatest show of gratitude is by investing your time in saying 'thank you'. In crazy, busy modern lives, an investment of time into saying 'thank you' in a special way is an uncommonly powerful expression of love for your partner.

The Perspective of Gratitude

Remembering the things you are grateful for gets you through some tough spots that require perspective. Your partner will not always be capable of providing the support you may need, as hard as they try. During these difficult times, remember why you are with them, the aspects of your relationship that are strong and keep you together. It is in this facility that gratitude, used to gain perspective, can become invaluable as it strengthens you during times of emotional weakness or duress.

Gratitude is one of the most powerful tools you have in a relationship. Using it to shore up emotional support, to provide positive feedback, and to remember what you're grateful for before rushing to judge your partner are all ways in which gratitude strengthens your bond. It may require time to take hold, but when it does it's the mortar that can seal the cracks that show up in everything over time.

Tip 23: Be Helpful

"The purpose of life is not to be happy. It is to be useful, to be honorable, to be compassionate, to have it make some difference that you have lived and lived well."
— Ralph Waldo Emerson

The concept of *quid pro qui* – something for something – should have no room in your relationship. While it's normal, and right, to expect fundamental things in your relationship such as emotional support and loyalty, it's another thing altogether to only be there for one another when we expect something in kind. When your relationship with your better half is feeling bleak, or even joyous, do lend a helping hand. Being helpful is, after all, tantamount to being loving. The beauty of love – and being helpful – is it sets the tone for mutual affection in any relationship, especially the intimate ones.

Be the First to Act

Being helpful is about being kind, and no relationship can last without kindness. If your partner is in a bad mood because of stress, use the opportunity to prove your love. Love is in the every day, in how we are there for one another.

What happens when you yourself are in a bad mood? Being helpful is not about looking over your shoulders to see what you can get. It is your responsibility to deal with your own bad mood. This isn't something your partner should try and fix. While the same holds true for the other person, the responsibility to make the decision to be loving and helpful when your loved one is feeling under the weather is also yours. When we expect other people to cater and adjust to our cycling moods, no progress can be made. Bad moods have a negative impact on everyone in the family. It's like an infectious disease that triggers additional negative emotions like anger, depression and anxiety. Everyone suffers.

A Loving Perspective

The key to reaching out to help even when you yourself feel in need is to remember love is more than a feeling. Real love transcends bad moods. Easier said than done, true. But also remember the beauty of love and how love given boomerangs back to us. Yes, not instantly all the time. Sometimes, not at all - at least not where immediate evidence is concerned. But acts of love go beyond seeking repayment. It's a spiritual endeavor that melts selfishness and pain in your own heart.

If your partner needs help with the chores because they had an extra stressful day at work but you'd rather sit in front of the TV, ask yourself, "Is an hour too much to ask of me? What satisfaction can I get from relaxing while deep down knowing I could have helped my partner?" Don't choose ephemeral delights over helpful and loving actions that will prove more beneficial to your relationship – and your own happiness and fulfillment – in the long haul. Think of how things would be different, too, if the tables were turned. How would you feel if you needed your partner but they chose to relax instead of lend you a helping hand? Sure, the thought of watching TV at the moment might be, or so you think, in line with your goal of feeling better, but for how long? Helping and loving your spouse involves making an investment in your important relationship, an investment that holds more than any monetary value.

Reaping What You Sow

You heard awful news from your sister and you need your partner to listen to you recount the sorry details. They, however, are up to their neck with a looming deadline. Someone has to cook dinner. Do you whine or nag in order to be heard? Do you resent your partner's work and the time it's taking away from you and your need for loving attention? These are all obviously negative ways to react. Think of being helpful in this scenario, and those like it, and, chances are, you can get the love that you want. How? By giving it. Offer to make dinner. Your significant other is more than likely going to appreciate the effort. Your chances of getting an attentive caring ear have just increased. If that's not the case, be happy knowing you've lessened some of the burdens of daily chores pressing on your partner's shoulders.

Wait for them to finish work and you probably won't have to complain about getting the attention that you desire. What's the point of using your other half as a sounding board now, only to be met with a resentful ear, and no dinner for the both of you? Being helpful, while a task that shouldn't be approached with the goal of getting something back, is love in action. And love will always beget love, even if it's not immediately observed.

While there is no magic guarantee that to love will get you the love you need, to love in itself is all you need. The giving of one's self is an unselfish act that is pure positivity. Positivity will attract more positivity in your life. When was the last time you acted like a selfish brat, gotten what you wanted, and deep down felt at peace and in tune with your inner self?

While love involves sacrifice and being helpful can be a mighty inconvenience at times, your relationship is sure to grow from the helpfulness and care you bestow upon your partner. When two people have the mindset of helping each other out, what happens is a beautiful cycle where two people can brave the storms of life with the assurance that their partner has their back. In a culture of pervasive narcissism, being helpful breaks through ugly dynamics where the mentality is "me, me, me". Being helpful is saying "I love you" in a way words can never portray.

Tip 24: Don't Over Compensate the Romance

"When you stop expecting people to be perfect, you can like them for who they are."
— Donald Miller

Over-romanticizing your relationship is a trap laying in wait for long-term unions. It's easy in the beginning to be swept off your feet by the romance of a new relationship. The thrill of a new paramour is rocket fuel for the stratospheric fresh relationship. But, it's not the kind of fuel that keeps a relationship alive and strong for a long time.

As time moves forward and a relationship grows, over-romanticizing can become tedious for both you and your partner. Making everything a grand romantic gesture is tiring, and not necessary for a strong couple. There will be certain milestones that are injections of romance, but romance is a sweetener, not a staple, of a long-term relationship and too much of it can be unhealthy.

The Honeymoon Phase

Typically, most relationships feature two pronounced 'honeymoon' phases where over-romanticizing everything occurs - the initial time after two people start a new relationship, and the time directly following a wedding or other explicitly expressed mutual agreement to stay committed for the long haul. These are wonderful, magic times of romance but they have an expiration date. When that expiration date is depends on you and your significant other. Some people keep that fire burning for over a year, others grow weary of that brand of romance after a day.

No matter how romantic your inclinations are, it's important to handle the transition to the more every-day relationship norms. This doesn't mean the elimination of romance, it means seeing what's there when the grand gestures and euphoric emotional high come to an end. Love encompasses both periods - the over-romantic days on special occasions and the normal day-to-day romance.

Comparative Romances

Making sure your relationship does not feel as though it's falling short during either period is vital to the emotional health of you and your partner. It can be uncomfortable for any new couple if you see other couples who are more - or less romantic - than you. What should be noted is that you and your partner are on the same page. If you're more pragmatic and prefer toned down expressions of love, that's okay. If you're a romantic pair who wants to take a week long scamper to a romantic destination, that's fine as well, just as long as you remember that you're in love during the weeks between those get-aways – that love and respect should exist in the doldrums of the everyday.

Don't compare notes with other people. You and your own partner have your own romantic dance to enjoy. The danger of comparing your romance with other romances is how you may open the door to letting external influences dictate the inner workings of your relationship. If your relationship is easily influenced by external factors, then maybe it's time to look to shoring up the bonds and strength of your relationship from the inside. Having stability is important, but so is romance. Balance is needed to maintain the relationship as the years roll by.

Open Communication

Communicating about your romantic needs is one way to ensure you don't feel overly wined-and-dined but neither ignored in your sweatpants with a TV dinner. Open, honest communication helps to keep a couple on the same page. Remember, it's always valuable to have something shared to look forward to, and a romantic date is an excellent way of sharing something private between the two of you. But, do maintain open communication to ensure it doesn't interfere with you or your partner's busy schedules and thereby create additional stress.

Romance can be an awkward topic as it's perceived as 'natural' and 'spontaneous' when, in fact, it's something you can actively work at just as easily, and sometimes even more easily, than a spontaneous tryst. But, the key is always open communication with your partner.

Finally, over-romanticizing sometimes creates a burden for your partner as they feel the need to reciprocate similar romantic gestures, leading to an almost arms-race feel to a relationship that will result in collapse. Romance is best done simply and openly with communication and sensitivity to the needs of your partner. Over-romanticizing brings additional pressure – pressure that's unrealistic and unnecessary. By putting too much emphasis on romance, you could very possibly be choosing the icing over the cake. A constant reminder of what truly counts – loyalty, eagerness to make the other person loved, active listening, compromise, and the like – is vital for the survival of your relationship, more vital than promises of trips to Paris or extravagant gifts.

Pop culture can be blamed for over-romanticizing relationships. Love songs make us think romance should feel like teenage love every day, brimming with intense hormones. Hollywood films depict perfect heroes and heroines who feel a surge of instant chemistry and everything just seems to fall into place for their relationship, where a happy ever after is a gift bestowed by the universe, instead of something that requires much labor and commitment. Remind yourselves these are works of fiction. In real life, love that lasts requires forgiveness, effort and honesty. As beautiful as emotions triggered by romantic gestures can be, there's nothing more beautiful than two people sticking by one another, no matter what curve balls life throws their way.

Tip 25: Relationships are not the place for nagging or nitpicking

"To say that one waits a lifetime for his soulmate to come around is a paradox. People eventually get sick of waiting, take a chance on someone, and by the art of commitment become soulmates, which takes a lifetime to perfect."
— Criss Jami

In any intimate and long-term relationship, there will be little and big annoyances for sure. Sometimes, what were once traits you admired about your mate ("I like how he's great with people and can really work a crowd.") morph into personality defects in your eyes ("He's such a terrible flirt!"). It can be in the mundane, like how she leaves a clutter in the bathroom before you head out, or more serious issues like addiction. Whatever your reasons for nagging your partner when you do, one thing is for sure: nagging is damaging to your relationship.

How is nagging different from healthy communication? In healthy communication, we watch our words because we realize that providing criticism is an art form in itself. We don't just freely dish out harsh or whiny words without any thought given as to how these verbal cues are to be received by our partners. No matter how validated you feel your complaints are, there is a right and wrong way to express your thoughts. With nagging, there is a repeated way the request or complaint is expressed. It can be seen as nit-picking, faultfinding, always complaining, and highly cynical. Emotions are high, or at least very irritated, when nagging is involved.

The Cons of Nagging

The recipient of the nagging tends to feel blamed and attacked. They can also sense they're being manipulated, insulted and unappreciated. When people nag, they typically find that eventually their partners stop listening to them, or go out of their way to avoid interactions. This is counterproductive and nobody wins when communication has broken down to nagging patterns. It's also normal for our partners to feel like we have taken on the role of the parent, and them a naughty child, when we nag. Not exactly the type of dynamic you would expect out of a healthy relationship. The last thing you want is to behave like a nagging parent while your partner takes on the form of a rebellious teenager.

The pitfalls of nagging aren't just experienced by the recipient either. If you find yourself nagging, chances are you will feel unheard and disrespected. This is truer if you are apt to repeat your requests while your partner distances themselves or simply pretends not to have heard you. Nagging can also quickly lead to an escalated situation with you and your partner engaging in an all-out fight. When one party feels disrespected – in the case of nagging, both parties usually end up feeling disrespected – tempers will rise and nobody wins. The fight then becomes more about the nagging than the actual underlying issues that brought on the nagging to begin with.

Nagging can raise questions in the relationship. You and your partner will start to wonder where the positive feelings have gone and maybe even question your compatibility. Instead of being glad to be together and look forward to enjoying each other's company, nagging can make you and your partner see each other as annoyances to be avoided or fought off.

Alternatives to Nagging

There's nothing fun or pleasant about nagging. So much time and energy are wasted by both parties. So how do you avoid nagging while having yourself heard? If you're the recipient of the nagging, there is a good chance your partner isn't aware they're doing this less-than-pleasant behavior. A gentle reminder might help if the tension hasn't reached the stage of being too thick. If your partner is way too irritated, it's best not to call them a nagger in the thick of things. A better approach is to let your partner know you have heard them and offer ways to meet their needs. If it's not immediately possible for you to act on whatever your other half is complaining about, remind them in a kind tone that you love them and that you're there to make things easier for the both of you. Never answer with a harsh tone. No matter how annoying and even hurtful nagging can be at times, compassion will go a long way. Keep in mind that your partner is on your case because they too are stressed out about something. Nobody truly wants to be nagging, after all. Perhaps your clutter is stressing them out to the point where they can't hold it in anymore, or maybe they're complaining about how forgetful you are because you truly can be inconsiderate. A good look at your own flaws is a sign of love. Don't focus on the nagging, but on the underlying reasons behind it.

If you find yourself to be the nagger, stop and think - Is what you're complaining about truly valid or can you let it slide? If it's really worth mentioning, don't be on your partner's case when emotions are strong. Find a way to relay your feelings without sounding critical and repetitive. Avoid "you" statements and generalizations. Statements like "You never take out the trash" or "You always forget what I ask you to do" are not going to work for your relationship. Focus on the positives like voicing out what you appreciate about your spouse – be it a trait or something they recently did – and express your needs gently afterwards. Do take on the positive reinforcement approach. Instead of criticizing your partner for being messy or forgetful, for example, tell them how happy you feel when they make an effort to be clean or bring up the last time your mate did something loving. Be sincere or you may come off as manipulative.

The main problem, as a whole, with nagging is the more you feel your needs aren't met, the more you tend to complain. The more you tend to complain (i.e. nag) the more your partner will feel the need to shut you off. By focusing on effective communication, active listening and appreciation, you and your significant other can nip nagging in the bud before it becomes a vicious cycle. Communicating in a healthy manner takes practice – plenty of it – but it's well worth the effort for you will be rewarded with a relationship that is open and warm, free from constant criticisms and putdowns.

Tip 26: Don't Lose Focus: Keep you Eyes on the Prize

"The true measure of success is how many times you can bounce back from failure."
— Stephen Richards

It's a fast-everything world – fast-food, high-speed Internet access, fast-paced lifestyles, and quick divorces. Purveyors of pop culture are often left wondering, "Where has the good – and real – music gone?" What happened to the bygone golden age of Hollywood where falling in love onscreen called for substantial emotional chemistry, and not simply two people jumping into bed with one another after a quick chance encounter? Porn is everywhere, morality isn't. Turn on your TV and you'll be fortunate to not be flashed with asinine shows where a materialistic lifestyle and chauvinistic behaviors are lauded while integrity and faithfulness take a backseat.

Committed relationships where loyalty and an attitude of "let's fix things instead of throw them away for a better model" are becoming more rare each passing day. True, people still stay glued to news about the royal wedding and happily-ever-after's promised in songs and films even up to this day, but how many of these individuals practice the same mindset in their actual lives? How many of us today stay true to the value of perseverance, of sticking it out through thick and thin?

This world and all its innovative conveniences have made certain things more difficult, albeit unintentionally. Communicating across distances is far easier now than ever before, so why do relationships fall apart at a faster rate than ever? Videos can be sent between lovers in a matter of seconds, but why do people throw away their time and give in the brutish calls of television, seedy websites and other mind-numbing digital distractions? There seems to be a war for our minds, a war for our attention. Money is to be made in this digital age and the perpetrators are getting more ruthless. How do old fashioned values like faithfulness, love for family and commitment stand a chance in this virtual age?

Mindfulness as an Art Form

Mindfulness is described as the conscious effort of accepting, in a non-judgmental way, the feelings and thoughts one is going through in the present moment. It's a form of meditation learned from Buddhist teachings. Whether you're into meditation or not, there is much to be learned from the concept of mindfulness. It's living in the "now", not in the to-do lists of tomorrows or the should-have-done of yesteryears.

Mindfulness is noticing and appreciating what you have, feel and sense in any given moment.

When it comes to your committed relationship, mindfulness can teach you the lesson of being present for your partner as you spend intimate moments together. Mindfulness calls for the shutting out of distractions – be it your phone, emails, and the like – when you're at home with your loved one. Mindfulness, by focusing on what you have at hand, also teaches us to work on what we have in our relationship, instead of giving into the distractions of what could be with other people. The lure of sex in media and the easy way humans today communicate open new doors of temptations. Mindfulness, being aware of where you are and what you have in life, tells you don't have to walk into those doors. The grass is green where you water it. While media tells us there are people who are younger and sexier and more exciting, mindfulness tells you to open your senses and appreciate the love you already have in your life.

Fighting Off Temptations

For any person in a loving and committed relationship, there will always be the existence of temptations. You can be in line at your local bank and the cute teller behind the counter smiles suggestively at you for the third time in a month. A co-worker sends you overtly friendly text messages and you can't help but feel flattered. Feeling flattered and liking the attention is as normal as the day is long. Your partner won't be immune to the lingering thoughts these unexpected attention and temptations bring as well. What's vital to keep in mind is that these are all normal experiences, experiences that should come and also go as quickly as they arrived.

Falling in love brings no guarantee that we won't find other people attractive, or that other people won't find us appealing simply because we have a ring on our finger or a long-term love everyone knows about. This is not surprising in a world where morals are questionable at best.

In the event where you start to entertain thoughts of giving in to temptation, take a huge step back. Is cheating really what you want in the long run, is it worth it to give in to an act that will horribly disfigure a relationship you and your partner have worked so hard to strengthen? A night spent with a fling might be sweet to the senses. But like all delicacies, they too will spoil. And, sadly, they won't spoil alone. Once you cross the boundary and give in to a sordid temptation – no matter how appealing – it can very well be a memory you and your partner can't just erase.

The world bombasts us with calls of how there are new horizons to conquer. Yes, we are ever so lucky information is so effortless to attain today. Technology does come with its many perks, after all. But the search for a human connection is as deeply ingrained in us as our need for food. If that was not so, technology in the likes of social media wouldn't have risen to the giants they are today. There is no substitute, however, for the real presence of somebody we know intimately, somebody we have experienced real life with. Appreciate what you have in the form of your partner. Do not make the mistake of many regretful souls before you who have lost the moon while searching for the stars.

Tip 27: Don't Be Selfish

"Selfishness is not living as one wishes to live, it is asking others to live as one wishes to live."
— Oscar Wilde

Selfishness is the opposite of giving. When we don't give ourselves – be it financially, emotionally, sexually – to our partners, we inhibit the flow of love in our relationship. Selfishness is one of the biggest enemies of love in a committed relationship, as well as love in any relationship for that matter. While we may be prone to sometimes think that to be selfish means we get more of what we want, the contrary is true. Our selfish nature deceives us into assuming that we can reap plenty of benefits from our lack of generosity, from a "me" first attitude towards others, including the person we promise to love and cherish. What happens, however, when we give in to our selfish desires is we end up turning upon ourselves.

The Effects of Selfishness

The lack of self-giving in the relationship leaves us eventually feeling void and unhappy at the very center of our soul. What transpires next is that a cancerous type of weakness wreaks havoc in the bond we should be sharing with our significant other. Selfishness is such a massive problem when it becomes a regular habit that it can lead to anger, addiction, infidelity and, yes, separation. Love is the bond that holds you and your partner together, the type of love that transcends feelings and gives root to good deeds. Selfishness is contrary to this bond and, in fact, damages the union that you two share. If you don't address perpetual selfish thoughts and habits that assail you, these can lead to the both of you treating each other like objects, rather than individuals to be respected and cherished.

Love attracts more love while selfishness repels others, especially your mate, from you. It can swiftly create a home where resentments and other hurt feelings abound. Communication breakdown can arise from this terrible habit as selfishness isn't just about hoarding material objects, although that is a very common and obvious symptom, it also involves being selfish towards the giving of your emotions. In healthy communication, there is a denial of self involved, such as denying yourself the urge to speak out when you know voicing a harsh opinion in the heat of an argument will just hurt your partner. When love isn't present and selfishness reigns, we fall into the habit of throwing hurtful verbal daggers when we are ever so inclined as we then lack the charity to hold our tongue for the sake of another. Selfishness, too, keeps you and your mate from growing together in your relationship. As love waters and nurtures your union, selfish habits are like weeds that inhibit the build-up of something beautiful, namely trust and joy.

Signs of Selfishness

Do you at times find it difficult to compromise with your partner, not because an actual compromise is difficult to come by – this can happen – but because your pride and ego keeps you from agreeing to a mutually beneficial solution with your mate? Do you have an "all about me" approach when it comes to decision-making in your relationship? Do you, despite what your gut tells you, withhold forgiving your partner because in doing so you will have to swallow your pride and look past their faults? Do you feel competitive towards your partner? Do you feel your partner owes you whenever you give something of yourself, be it time, money, affection or anything else that requires effort? These are all signs of selfishness. Selfishness could take the form of withholding financial support to a partner who truly needs it, refusing to share material goods. This type of selfishness is what usually comes to mind when the subject is discussed. While these are true examples of selfish behaviors, be on the lookout of lesser known habits that reflect a lack of generosity and love in your relationship.

Overcoming the Selfish Beast

Dealing with selfishness within us and in our spouse is no easy feat. As humans we are all hardwired with self-preservation. Just like giving in to lustful or gluttonous desires might feel natural yet leave us feeling empty and suffering the consequences of our actions, submitting to selfishness like an animal would to instinct comes with a whole slew of consequences.

You can't control the actions, including selfish ones, in your spouse so the best approach to combating selfishness in your relationship is to look within yourself and pinpoint your own selfish tendencies. This is the first step in eradicating the ugly face of selfishness in your life. Be responsible and honestly admit your own selfish nature. A good question to ask yourself when dealing with your spouse, especially when decisions have to be made, is "Is this what's best for the two of us, or just me?" Another step towards the right direction in removing the roots of selfishness in your live is to look into the main cause of financial issues. Do you and your partner have money problems due to you wanting to spend more on things you desire but don't need?

When addressing selfish behaviors, this is a great time to communicate with your partner and work on ways you both can compromise. Accept that you alone no longer function as one person but as part of a team. Whatever you do will affect another person's life. In removing selfishness from your own self, you need to change the thinking process of "me" to "we".

Patience is a key component here as self-love and preservation aren't concepts that will dissipate overnight. This is one of those moments where the journey has to be regarded as opposed to a utopian destination. When the voice of the spoiled toddler takes over your thinking the next time you interact with your partner, when the "I want, I want!" in you screams, it pays to remember that selfishness, far from adding to your own personal fulfillment and happiness, will erode your relationship and own serenity.

Tip 28: Associate with the Right People

"I would rather walk with a friend in the dark, than alone in the light."
— Helen Keller

When we're in committed relationships, we share a life with someone else. In the most committed unions such as marriage, couples are often advised to be like "one", a union so intimate that they should operate as a single entity. This doesn't mean to say, however, that anyone in a serious relationship should act like an island and block out everyone else who's not their partner. Having friends is a healthy part of being a couple. Friends can bring us out of ourselves, our routines, including unhealthy patterns, and our worries. The company of other people can provide us much laughter, cherished memories, and additional opportunities to learn and grow. Friends can share with us insights to the world that we, even as a team in a relationship, can't achieve on our own.

Steering Clear of the Negative

This is not to say, though, that all friendships are healthy. Just like our friendships with other people can positively affect us and our lives, these too can have a negative impact on the relationship we hold most dear. There is such a thing as inappropriate or "dangerous" friendships.

These can include friendships with the opposite sex that involve putting yourself in situations that can destroy your relationship with your romantic partner. Some people scoff at the idea of friends posing any danger to their romantic relationships, citing trust as the key issue and solution. But let's be realistic. Spending time with friends that you may eventually find attractive or who may one day find you appealing – if the attraction hasn't occurred yet – is asking for trouble. While common thoughts of affairs might involve the husband who seeks one-night-stands at bars, or the depressed girlfriend who seeks for further emotional connection and validation through online dating, most people don't realize how common seemingly innocuous friendships transform into full-blown affairs.

Setting boundaries and being realistic can be the way to approach friendships with other people without completely eliminating them from your life. The boundary can involve interacting with friends as a couple, instead of spending time alone with them as individuals. With the many factors and varying elements in life, one can never be too sure in assuming that nothing inappropriate can occur from friendships. Sometimes all it takes for a disastrous episode involving a friend is a stressful week, a partner who's away for whatever valid reason, and a friendly neighbor who invites you or your partner for a drink, just as "friends". Staying realistic and within mutually agreed upon boundaries can save you and your mate from tremendous heartache.

Building Strong Bonds

Aside from the pains of infidelity, there are other ways friendships can negatively affect your romantic relationship. Of course, the solution of removing people completely from your lives as a couple is not a healthy one either. Just like investing in friendships with like-minded people can boost your morale better than hanging out with individuals who have hobbies and lifestyles contrary to yours, spending time with other couples is healthier for your relationship with your significant other rather than with single people. Other couples can provide a healthier and safer atmosphere for socializing as you can all make plans as a group. This not only significantly lessens the risk of inappropriate friendships, you and your partner furthermore will have the opportunity to bond with people whose lifestyles and mentality are closer to your own.

Who can understand the joys and issues you and your partner enjoy and tackle on a regular basis more than other couples? Single friends, no matter how much we enjoy their company and shouldn't completely remove them from our lives, will have a different mindset. Whether these single buddies are on the lookout for a mate or are enjoying their singlehood in bliss, they will most likely have different schedules and idea of a fun time. And while not all single people are miserable in their being alone, it's not rare either to have single pals who may be looking at your committed relationship with envy. After all, envy usually doesn't live far away. The last thing you need is a friend who masks their intentions and tries to manipulate you into thinking you could have it better with someone else or as a single person yourself.

Even well-meaning single friends could leave you feeling empty. Committed relationships are such complicated entities that someone who isn't in one won't be able to really relate to you and your partner in a way that is healthy and beneficial for your bond. These single pals won't be able to provide you with personal insights based on real situations they themselves go through, experiences that you can gather much knowledge and strength from. They may have a cavalier nonchalant approach to your romantic relationship as you open up and share your joys and sorrows, or, worse, they can possess a rather cynical approach and offer you Tip that implies giving up on your relationship and seek happiness elsewhere.

This is not to say all single friends are to be avoided. Simply take these as cautions to keep in mind. If you have single friends who have always been supportive of your romantic relationship, by all means keep them close (within healthy boundaries, of course). Likewise, if you have friends who themselves are in committed relationships but only continue to add negative fodder to your own relationship, it's best to steer clear and seek the company of more supportive friends with your mate. One beauty of friends is we get to choose them, so choose wisely. Surround yourself and your partner with people who are supportive and who help your relationship grow in the healthy way it's supposed to.

Tip 29: Avoid Geographical Cures

"Always focus on the front windshield and not the review mirror."
— Colin Powell

Like a ghost, our emotional baggage – from fears to personality defects, resentments and the like – will follow us wherever we go. While thoughts of relocating to a new place or finding a new partner can hit the best of us at times, there is no such thing as a geographical cure when fundamental issues within ourselves are the true culprit affecting our relationship and personal serenity.

Seeking a geographical cure is way to hide from reality. The reality we face can be issues in our relationship to, more often than not, issues within ourselves. What makes you think a new city will take away the emptiness rooted deep inside you? How can a new environment change the addiction you haven't addressed, or the anger you continue to fail to control? A new address won't take away the resentments you still hold, the unwanted gifts from the past. Neither will a new partner or a new apartment, no matter how appealing from the outside, dissipate the selfishness, lack of self-control, negative outlook or whatever character defect resides within your psyche.

Attempting to change locations to cure the ill inside you or in your relationship is actually a form of denial. It's an unhealthy and ineffective defense mechanism in which you attempt to run from something that is too uncomfortable to bear and accept. You can try to convince yourself that your problems are external, that you won't be fighting so much with your spouse if you lived somewhere else, or if they were someone else. To a certain degree in certain circumstances, maybe a change of scenery can prove beneficial, but always only to a limited degree. What assails you from inside, your flaws and fears, cannot be remedied by a change of address.

An escape sounds like the easiest solution at the moment, especially when tensions are high and you think you've reached the end of your sanity. But there is no escaping a problem that is rooted inside you. The key is to stay true to yourself and address the issues right where they are. If you have problems with anger management, seek professional help, not a new zip code. If you can't handle your finances, read the best self-help books on money management you can find and practice what you learn. A new condo won't address the issue of how you can't properly balance your pay check and expenses. Woe to you if you expect a new partner will heal you of your childhood hurts, or melt away your propensity to pick up the bottle when life once more assails you with a new problem to tackle.

What happens when you escape problems by changing the external rather than the internal is you will find yourself in unhealthy patterns that can last years, if not a lifetime. Hopping from one job to the next, or moving from one city to the next exciting locale, becomes a habit. It happens all the time. Plenty of people – out of fear, or denial, or pride, or all three – refuse to look within themselves for the character defects that cause their problems. Instead, they would rather blame external circumstances. "I would be happier if I lived in New York". "I wouldn't smoke so much if my partner was more sympathetic."

Making excuses for our own actions is a form of denial. As little children we learn to blame. "He hit me first!" or "She said so and I just followed." Healthy adults grow out of the blame game, plenty of us don't. Making excuses and convincing ourselves and others that we're fine and the problem lies elsewhere is, in reality, a form of copping out. We utter excuses like, "If you were married to him you'd understand," or "If you've gone through what I've experienced…"

Do you really want to be a victim of external circumstances, circumstances beyond your control? Rather than play the victim card, take the reins and manage your problems from where you actually have control: inside yourself. We can't control the actions of other people, but we can definitely choose how to react to circumstances. Even our own feelings can leave us feeling helpless. Thankfully, we are more than our feelings. We are what we do.

When the going gets rough and you find yourself thinking that what you need is a fresh start somewhere else, or with someone else, remind yourself you need to be honest and have an in-depth look at what's inside of you. Jumping to a new location or a new relationship without a rigorous assessment of your own contribution to the problems will lead you to unfortunately discover the problems have followed you to where you've gone.

Be true to yourself and continue to always seek self-improvement. It's an effort that has to be done throughout life, but it's an endeavor with its own set of beautiful rewards. There is a saying that goes, "No Matter Where You Go, There You Are!" Work on how you live, not where you live.

Tip 30: Don't Give up Before the Miracle Happens

"Courage doesn't always roar, sometimes it's the quiet voice at the end of the day whispering 'I will try again tomorrow"
— Mary Anne Radmacher

It's common knowledge that committed relationships take plenty of effort. This is a healthy and realistic approach. Unfortunately, it's also a common belief that there is such a thing as only one perfect person out there. The notion of that one ideal person is dangerous because it holds up an unrealistic romantic expectation that a long-term relationship will be successful because we've found the perfect mate, as opposed to putting in the work to nurture a relationship. Pretty soon, people who think they found the perfect man or woman discover that real gritty work is involved in sticking to their vows. Some then assume that since their relationship has met resistance through normal conflicts, they have committed to the wrong person.

The first step you must undertake is to accept the fact that while being in a committed relationship has its joys and blessings, the bond you share can often be difficult and complicated. What you have are two people with two separate backgrounds coming together to share one life. Of course conflicts are natural. Walking hand in hand into the future together will involve bickering and even occasions of loneliness.

Being in love is one of the sweetest emotions yet it's not wise to underestimate the feelings of anxiety, fear and anger that accompany intimate relationships. If you encounter any of these in your union, you are not alone. You haven't made the mistake of committing to the wrong person – except, of course, in the case of abuse, cruelty and abandonment. The ups and downs of relationships can, and will most definitely, happen to everyone.

When dealing with problems in your relationship, you may at times feel like giving up. The grass will appear greener on some other side. The thought of perhaps a sweeter and more attentive partner will tempt you. Even the thought of being single will sometimes sound plenty more attractive than working through the myriad of problems you share with your partner. Again, remember these are normal emotions and are not indicative of you choosing the wrong mate. Another healthy approach before taking the path away from your relationship is adopting the attitude that you can only change yourself. In your relationship, you control your own half and nothing else. Eliminate the victim mentality. The blame game gets old and will accomplish you nothing but more sorrow, especially once you realize you are feeling low based on factors you have no control over. Even in the event that you decide you want to take a break for it and remove yourself from the relationship, you still won't be able to escape your own flaws. The responsibility of being the best person you can be, single or not, will continue to fall on your shoulders and your shoulders alone.

While it's no easy feat to deal with relationship issues, some studies have shown that couples who stay and cope can usually restore their bond and even end up happier than before. Yes, the pain you experiences is real – whether it was in the form of betrayal, constant arguments, cold shoulders and very heated words. You have every right to feel hurt. But ending a committed relationship will also have its own set of pains and hurts. Unless there's abuse involved, keep in mind that getting out of your commitment and ending a life shared with your partner can open the door to loneliness, resentments and regrets. Starting a new relationship without addressing your own defects will result in a repeat performance. Some people even find they have jumped out of the furnace and into the fire.

Relationships evolve. Being unhappy in your relationship now doesn't automatically mean to say you will be unhappy with the same person forever. When there's willingness to improve and forgive, you and your partner can definitely work through your kinks and personal flaws. Starting over with someone else simply means that: starting over. Gone will be the emotional investment you've placed in the person you're with now. Giving up involves turning your back on the successes, no matter how small and spaced out they may seem right now, you've enjoyed with your partner.

Before you throw in the towel, exhaust all options. Give yourself and your partner the gift of endurance. Seek professional help, read positive self-help materials, adjust the way you deal with conflict and, above all, put your partner before yourself. Transforming your union from one that is besought with problems to one that is brimming with joy is accomplished one day at a time, one loving gesture at a time.

Saying goodbye now is also saying goodbye to what could be. All the work you both put into making your relationship work are like seeds that should be nurtured. Oak trees, gorgeous and sturdy specimens of nature that survive for decades, don't show up on our lawns overnight. In the same way, your relationship will need patience through the storms before it can bestow you with its many fruits - Don't give up before the miracle happens.

www.ingramcontent.com/pod-product-compliance
Lightning Source LLC
Chambersburg PA
CBHW071508040426
42444CB00008B/1543